Contents

KT-573-664

AB
657
H 38900
£18°°

AAT

ernal Auditing

Level 4

onal Diploma in
Accounting

Course Book

For assessments from
September 2017

Second edition 2017

ISBN 9781 5097 1214 4
ISBN (for internal use only) 9781 5097 1233 5

British Library Cataloguing-in-Publication Data
A catalogue record for this book is available from the
British Library

Published by

BPP Learning Media Ltd
BPP House, Aldine Place
142-144 Uxbridge Road
London W12 8AA

www.bpp.com/learningmedia

Printed in the United Kingdom

Your learning materials, published by BPP Learning Media
Ltd, are printed on paper obtained from traceable
sustainable sources.

The contents of this course material are intended as a guide
and not professional advice. Although every effort has been
made to ensure that the contents of this course material are
correct at the time of going to press, BPP Learning Media
makes no warranty that the information in this course
material is accurate or complete and accept no liability for
any loss or damage suffered by any person acting or
refraining from acting as a result of the material in this
course material.

BPP Learning Media is grateful to the IASB for permission to
reproduce extracts from the International Financial Reporting
Standards including all International Accounting Standards,
SIC and IFRIC Interpretations (the Standards). The Standards
together with their accompanying documents are issued by:

The International Accounting Standards Board (IASB) 30
Cannon Street, London, EC4M 6XH, United Kingdom. Email:
info@ifrs.org Web: www.ifrs.org

Disclaimer: The IASB, the International Financial Reporting
Standards (IFRS) Foundation, the authors and the publishers
do not accept responsibility for any loss caused by acting or
refraining from acting in reliance on the material in this
publication, whether such loss is caused by negligence or
otherwise to the maximum extent permitted by law.

Introduction to the course

Syllabus overview

This unit is about external audits of financial statements, which are undertaken in accordance with International Standards on Auditing, to provide assurance to the intended users as to the credibility of the information contained within the financial statements.

The unit is designed to equip students with the knowledge and skills required to undertake an external audit under supervision. It is directed at students who wish to pursue a career in an accountancy firm that undertakes external audits. However, the coverage of accounting systems, internal controls and the control environment will provide those students wishing to pursue a career in finance or internal audit in any organisation with a strong foundation in governance procedures.

On completion of this unit, students will:

- Understand the essence and objectives of the audit process, and the ethical and professional implications of the regulatory requirements and pronouncements of the professional bodies

- Understand the nature and importance of internal controls and identify deficiencies in accounting systems

- Be able to contribute to the conduct of all stages of an external audit, including planning, gathering sufficient appropriate evidence, and concluding and reporting findings in accordance with International Standards on Auditing (ISA).

Test specification for this unit assessment

Assessment method	Marking type	Duration of assessment
Computer based assessment	Partially computer/ partially human marked	2 hours

Learning outcomes		Weighting
1	Demonstrate an understanding of the principles of auditing	5%
2	Demonstrate the importance of professional ethics	12%
3	Evaluate the audited entity's system of internal control	15%
4	Evaluate audit procedures for obtaining audit evidence	15%
5	Evaluate the planning process	33%
6	Evaluate audit procedures	20%
Total		**100%**

Assessment structure

2 hours duration

Competency is 70%

*Note that this is only a guideline as to what might be tested. The format and content of each task may vary from what we have listed below.

Your assessment will consist of 23 tasks.

Task	Expected content	Max marks	Chapter ref	Study complete
Task 1	**Demonstrate an appreciation of the concept of assurance** • The difference between reasonable and limited assurance • The difference between positive and negative expression of assurance • The benefits gained from assurance • The meaning of true and fair view/presents fairly.	2	Chapter 1	
Task 2	**Discuss the objectives of audits conducted under International Standards on Auditing (ISA)** • The respective responsibilities of management and external auditors in relation to the financial statements • The role of professional scepticism and professional judgement • Elements of a report to management on deficiencies in internal control • Elements of the auditor's report • The contents of adequate accounting records • The role of the International Auditing and Assurance Standards Board (IAASB).	3	Chapter 1	

Task	Expected content	Max marks	Chapter ref	Study complete

Task 3	**Identify the principles and characteristics of ethical codes and the implications for the auditor**
	
	• The consequences of failing to comply with the AAT Code of Professional Ethics, including damages, and legal and professional penalties
	
	• The auditor's liability to the company and shareholders under contract, and liability to third parties under tort of negligence
	
	• The need for professional indemnity insurance
	
	• How liability can be limited through use of:
	  – Limited liability agreements between auditor and client (proportionate liability and liability cap)
	  – Limited liability partnerships
	  – Disclaimer of liability (Bannerman clause).
		3	Chapter 1	

Task	Expected content	Max marks	Chapter ref	Study complete
Task 4	**Consider threats to the fundamental ethical principles and the independence of auditors** • The fundamental principles of integrity, objectivity, professional competence and due care, confidentiality and professional behaviour, as set out in the AAT Code of Professional Ethics • The significance of independence and its relationship with objectivity • The threats of self-interest, self-review, advocacy, familiarity and intimidation • Circumstances that threaten the application of the fundamental principles.	4	Chapter 1	

Task	Expected content	Max marks	Chapter ref	Study complete
Task 5	**Evaluate safeguards to eliminate or reduce threats to the fundamental ethical principles and the independence of auditors** Evaluate firm-wide safeguards: • The use of different personnel with different reporting lines for the provision of non-assurance services to an audited entity • Procedures for monitoring and managing the reliance on revenue received from a single client • Procedures that will enable the identification of interests or relationships between the firm or members of the engagement team and clients • Disciplinary mechanisms to promote compliance with policies and procedures Evaluate engagement-specific safeguards: • Independent review of audit working papers • Consultation with an independent third party • Disclosure and discussion of ethical issues with those charged with governance • Rotation of senior personnel Evaluate matters that should be referred to senior members of audit staff.	2	Chapter 1	

Task	Expected content	Max marks	Chapter ref	Study complete
Task 6	**Apply the fundamental principle of confidentiality** • Recognise when to disclose information with or without clients' permission. • Recognise when to take precautions if acting for competing clients.	3	Chapter 1	
Task 7	**Demonstrate an understanding of the principles of internal control** • The definition of internal control and each of its components (control environment, control activities, including performance reviews, information processing, physical controls, segregation of duties and monitoring of controls by management and/or an internal audit function) • Preventative and detective controls • Limitations of internal controls • Factors relating to the operating environment and internal control system that influence control risk.	3	Chapter 2	
Task 8	**Identify the main features of an accounting system** • Control objectives • Risks • Control procedures for the major accounting systems (purchases, revenue, payroll, inventory, non-current assets, bank and cash).	3	Chapter 2	

Task	Expected content	Max marks	Chapter ref	Study complete
Task 9	**Evaluate the effectiveness of an accounting control system** • Use systems records (flowcharts, internal control questions and checklists) to evaluate internal control systems • Use the evaluation of internal controls to determine the audit strategy • Identify the merits and limitations of using standardised questionnaires and checklists • Identify the factors that contribute to strengths and deficiencies in accounting systems.	5	Chapter 2	
Task 10	**Identify how internal controls mitigate risks** • Identify the types of errors and irregularities that can occur in accounting systems • Identify how errors and irregularities can be prevented or detected by control procedures.	4	Chapter 2	

Task	Expected content	Max marks	Chapter ref	Study complete
Task 11	**Evaluate methods used to obtain audit evidence in a given situation** • Types of verification techniques (inspection, observation, external confirmation, recalculation, re-performance, analytical procedures and enquiry) • When it is appropriate to use each type of verification technique • Reliability of different sources of audit evidence • Differences between tests of controls and substantive procedures • Methods used to test controls, transactions and balances • Assertions.	4	Chapter 3	
Task 12	**Evaluate audit techniques used in an IT environment** • Use computer-assisted audit techniques (CAATs), including test data, integrated test facilities and audit software, to test controls and interrogate the audited entity's files • Identify the benefits and drawbacks of using CAATs.	2	Chapter 3	

Task	Expected content	Max marks	Chapter ref	Study complete
Task 13	**Evaluate and use different sampling techniques** • Distinguish between statistical and non-statistical sampling • Determine when it is more appropriate to examine 100% or a selection of items • Distinguish between selection methods and when they should be used • Identify factors affecting sample sizes • Identify appropriate populations from which to select samples.	4	Chapter 3	
Task 14	**Develop an audit approach suitable for a given situation** • Establish why auditors need to understand the audited entity's internal controls • Determine when to use a mixture of tests of controls and substantive procedures or substantive procedures only • Identify why it is appropriate to use a mixture of tests of controls and substantive procedures or substantive procedures only.	3	Chapter 3	
Task 15	**Select procedures for a given assertion** • Apply audit procedures to test financial statement assertions.	2	Chapter 3	

Task	Expected content	Max marks	Chapter ref	Study complete
Task 16	**Demonstrate an understanding of how audit risk applies to external auditing** • The components of the audit risk model, inherent, control and detection risks (sampling and non-sampling risk) • The relationship between the components, in particular, how auditors manage detection risk in order to keep audit risk at an acceptably low level • How factors such as the entity's operating environment and its system of internal control affect the assessment of inherent and control risk • How analytical procedures can be used to identify potential under/overstatement of items in the financial statements.	10	Chapter 4	
Task 17	**Demonstrate how the concept of materiality applies to external auditing** • The difference between 'performance materiality' and 'materiality for the financial statements as a whole' • The role of materiality in planning an audit and evaluating misstatements • Methods used to calculate materiality thresholds • The difference between 'material' and 'material and pervasive'.	3	Chapter 4	

Task	Expected content	Max marks	Chapter ref	Study complete
Task 18	**Analyse the key audit risks for a given situation** Analyse factors relating to a given audited entity's operating environment and system of internal control give rise to risk of material misstatement in the financial statements.	10	Chapter 5	
Task 19	**Apply audit procedures to achieve audit objectives** Develop procedures to obtain sufficient appropriate evidence in respect of the relevant assertions for key figures in the financial statements, in particular: • Non-current assets • Inventory • Receivables • Cash and bank • Borrowings • Payables • Provisions • Revenue • Payroll and other expenses • Accruals and prepayments.	10	Chapter 5	
Task 20	**Examine the role of audit working papers** • The role of audit documentation in providing evidence as a basis for the auditor's opinion • The importance of retaining working papers for future reference • The form and content of working papers.	3	Chapter 6	

Task	Expected content	Max marks	Chapter ref	Study complete

Task 21	**Select and justify matters to be referred to a senior colleague**
	
	• Identify material and immaterial misstatements
	
	• Identify deviations from an audited entity's prescribed procedures
	
	• Identify matters of unusual nature and unauthorised transactions, unusual events:
	
	  – Non-routine transactions
	
	  – Related party transactions
	
	  – Transactions above or below market rates
	
	  – Suspected fraud.
		3	Chapter 6	

Task 22	**Effectively report audit findings to management** Identify the consequences of deficiencies in internal controls and how the deficiencies can be remedied.	10	Chapter 6	
Task 23	**Evaluate audit evidence and recommend a suitable audit opinion** Identify a suitable audit opinion arising from: • Significant uncertainties • Material misstatements • Inability to obtain sufficient, appropriate evidence (limitation on scope).	4	Chapter 6	

Skills bank

Our experience of preparing students for this type of assessment suggests that to obtain competency, you will need to develop a number of key skills.

What do I need to know to do well in the assessment?

It requires good overall awareness of many parts of your AAT studies so far and should be seen as an ideal way of applying much of what you have already learned as context for the new content that you will see, showing how audits are conducted in practice.

To be successful in the assessment you need to:

- Know the new material introduced in each chapter, having practised a number of tasks that reflect the real assessment.

- Apply the techniques demonstrated to 'real life' situations as presented in each task. These will mostly be tested using scenarios where you can consider what would really happen if you were the auditor.

Assumed knowledge

External Auditing is one of the **optional** Level 4 units. You need to understand the two Level 2 units, *Bookkeeping Transactions and Bookkeeping Controls*, and the two Level 3 units *Advanced Bookkeeping and Final Accounts*, and *Financial Statements of Limited Companies*, covered at Level 4, before taking this unit. At Level 4, the coverage of internal controls in the *External Auditing* unit will reinforce the knowledge and skills required in *Accounting Systems and Controls*.

Assessment style

In the assessment you could complete tasks by:

1   Entering narrative by selecting from drop down menus of narrative options known as **picklists**

2   Using **drag and drop** menus to enter narrative

3   Typing in numbers, known as **gapfill** entry

4   Entering **ticks**

5   Entering text by **writing an answer** to a discursive requirement (there are THREE such tasks in your assessment).

You must familiarise yourself with the style of the online questions and the AAT software before taking the assessment. As part of your revision, login to the **AAT website** and attempt their **online practice assessments**.

Answering written questions

In your assessment there will be written questions based on a given scenario. The main verbs used for these questions are as follows, along with their meanings:

Identify – Analyse and select for presentation

Explain – Set out in detail the meaning of

Recommend – Provide a solution

Topic areas that you might encounter in your assessment include:

- Identifying and explaining audit risks
- Setting out audit procedures
- Preparing extracts for a report

Before answering the question set, you need to read the scenario carefully to make sure that you identify the relevant points.

Introduction to the assessment

The question practice you do will prepare you for the format of tasks you will see in the *External Auditing* assessment. It is also useful to familiarise yourself with the introductory information you **may** be given at the start of the assessment. For example:

Each task is independent. You will not need to refer to your answers to previous tasks.

Read every task carefully to make sure you understand what is required.

Where the date is relevant, it is given in the task data.

Both minus signs and brackets can be used to indicate negative numbers UNLESS task instructions say otherwise.

You must use a full stop to indicate a decimal point. For example, write 100.57 NOT 100,57 OR 100 57.

You may use a comma to indicate a number in the thousands, but you don't have to. For example, 10000 and 10,000 are both OK.

Other indicators are not compatible with the computer-marked system.

Complete all 23 tasks

---

1   As you revise, use the **BPP Passcards** to consolidate your knowledge. They are a pocket-sized revision tool, perfect for packing in that last-minute revision.

2   Attempt as many tasks as possible in the **Question Bank**. There are plenty of assessment-style tasks which are excellent preparation for the real assessment.

3   Always **check** through your own answers as you will in the real assessment, before looking at the solutions in the back of the Question Bank.

Key to icons

 Key term

A key definition which is important to be aware of for the assessment

 Formula to learn

A formula you will need to learn as it will not be provided in the assessment

 Formula provided

A formula which is provided within the assessment and generally available as a pop-up on screen

 Activity

An example which allows you to apply your knowledge to the technique covered in the Course Book. The solution is provided at the end of the chapter

 Illustration

A worked example which can be used to review and see how an assessment question could be answered

 Assessment focus point

A high priority point for the assessment

 Open book reference

Where use of an open book will be allowed for the assessment

 Real life examples

A practical real life scenario

AAT qualifications

The material in this book may support the following AAT qualifications:

AAT Professional Diploma in Accounting Level 4, AAT Professional Diploma in Accounting at SCQF Level 8 and Certificate: Accounting (Level 5 AATSA).

Supplements

From time to time we may need to publish supplementary materials to one of our titles. This can be for a variety of reasons, from a small change in the AAT unit guidance to new legislation coming into effect between editions.

You should check our supplements page regularly for anything that may affect your learning materials. All supplements are available free of charge on our supplements page on our website at:

www.bpp.com/learning-media/about/students

Improving material and removing errors

There is a constant need to update and enhance our study materials in line with both regulatory changes and new insights into the assessments.

From our team of authors BPP appoints a subject expert to update and improve these materials for each new edition.

Their updated draft is subsequently technically checked by another author and from time to time non-technically checked by a proof reader.

We are very keen to remove as many numerical errors and narrative typos as we can but given the volume of detailed information being changed in a short space of time we know that a few errors will sometimes get through our net.

We apologise in advance for any inconvenience that an error might cause. We continue to look for new ways to improve these study materials and would welcome your suggestions. Please feel free to contact our AAT Head of Programme at nisarahmed@bpp.com if you have any suggestions for us.

Principles of auditing and professional ethics

Learning outcomes

1.1	**Demonstrate an appreciation of the concept of assurance**
	• Difference between reasonable and limited assurance
	• Difference between positive and negative expression of assurance
	• Benefits gained from assurance
	• Meaning of true and fair view/presents fairly.
1.2	**Discuss the objectives of audits conducted under International Standards on Auditing (ISA)**
	• The respective responsibilities of management and external auditors in relation to the financial statements
	• The role of professional scepticism and professional judgement
	• Elements of a report to management on deficiencies in internal control
	• Elements of the auditor's report
	• Contents of adequate accounting records
	• The role of the International Auditing and Assurance Standards Board (IAASB).
2.1	**Identify the principles and characteristics of ethical codes and the implications for the auditor**
	• The consequences of failing to comply with the AAT Code of Professional Ethics, including damages, and legal and professional penalties
	• The auditor's liability to the company and shareholders under contract, and liability to third parties under tort of negligence
	• The need for professional indemnity insurance
	• How liability can be limited through use of:
	– Limited liability agreements between auditor and client (proportionate liability and liability cap)
	– Limited liability partnerships
	– Disclaimer of liability (Bannerman clause).

2.2	Consider threats to the fundamental ethical principles and the independence of auditors
	• The fundamental principles of integrity, objectivity, professional competence and due care, confidentiality and professional behaviour, as set out in the AAT Code of Professional Ethics
	• The significance of independence and its relationship with objectivity
	• The threats of self-interest, self-review, advocacy, familiarity and intimidation
	• Circumstances that threaten the application of the fundamental principles.
2.3	Evaluate safeguards to eliminate or reduce threats to the fundamental ethical principles and the independence of auditors
	• Evaluate firm-wide safeguards:
	– Use of different personnel with different reporting lines for the provision of non-assurance services to an audited entity
	– Procedures for monitoring and managing the reliance on revenue received from a single client
	– Procedures that will enable the identification of interests or relationships between the firm or members of the engagement team and clients
	– Disciplinary mechanisms to promote compliance with policies and procedures
	• Evaluate engagement-specific safeguards:
	– Independent review of audit working papers
	– Consultation with an independent third party
	– Disclosure and discussion of ethical issues with those charged with governance
	– Rotation of senior personnel
	• Evaluate matters that should be referred to senior members of audit staff.
2.4	Apply the fundamental principle of confidentiality
	• Recognise when to disclose information with or without clients' permission
	• Recognise when to take precautions if acting for competing clients.

Assessment context

This topic introduces a number of terms that you will see examined as part of the *External Auditing* assessment. The contents of this topic make up six tasks in the assessment, so it is crucial that you understand the concepts discussed and how they could be examined.

Qualification context

Although there are some terms here that you may be familiar with from earlier parts of your AAT studies (such as ethics and company law), you may need to consider the context in which they are examined.

Business context

While seen as an unnecessary expense for a number of organisations, the bureaucracy and 'red tape' attached to being incorporated and then audited can help to provide a degree of confidence to the many stakeholders of a company. This topic will start to address the confidence or assurance provided by auditors, especially when their ethical credibility has been reinforced by adhering to a code of ethics.

Chapter overview

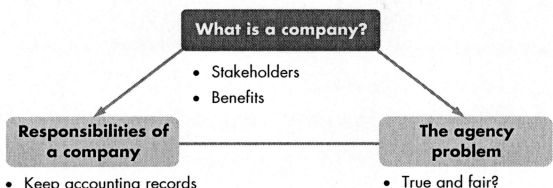

What is a company?

- Stakeholders
- Benefits

Responsibilities of a company

- Keep accounting records
- Provide financial statements

The agency problem

- True and fair?
- The solution? – Audit

What is an audit?

- Audit appointments
- Exemptions
- Benefits of an audit

ISA 200

- Regulation (IAASB and FRC)
- Responsibilities
- Professional liability and negligence
- Audit failure
- Restriction of liability
- Assurance
- Fraud
- Judgement
- Evidence
- Reporting

AAT Code of Professional Ethics

- Independence
- Fundamental principles (PIPCO)
- Conceptual framework (ASIFS)
- Safeguards
- Confidentiality and conflicts of interest

1 What is a company?

A company is an **organisation** set up ('incorporated') for a **specific purpose**, usually commercial. It is a separate legal entity and is registered under a piece of UK legislation called the **Companies Act 2006**.

A company may be viewed like this – a collection of related **stakeholders**:

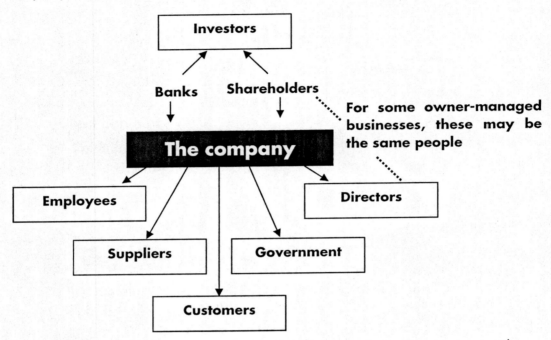

Registration under the Companies Act 2006 provides a company with specific **rights** but also forces upon it certain **responsibilities**, both of which we shall look at now.

1.1 Benefits of being a company

Companies are incorporated for many reasons. One of these reasons is the concept of **limited legal liability** where, in the event of any losses suffered by the company, the most that any investor can ever lose by being involved with that company is their investment. The company is consequently a separate legal entity from its shareholders.

2 Responsibilities of being a company

The Companies Act 2006 has over 1,300 different sections and covers over 750 pages of text, so a company's duties are **too numerous** to mention in full! However, there are two that are of particular interest to you for this course:

- The duty to keep **accounting records** (Companies Act 2006: s.386)
- The need to provide **financial statements** (Companies Act 2006: s.394)

2.1 Duty to keep accounting records

Section 386 of the Companies Act 2006 specifies the responsibilities of a company regarding the accounting records that must be kept.

Activity 1: Companies Act

Listed below are extracts from Section 386 of the Companies Act 2006.

Required

For each item highlighted, suggest a suitable example or accounting record.

(1) Every company must keep adequate accounting records.

(2) Adequate accounting records means records that are sufficient:

    (a) To show and explain the company's transactions

    (b) To disclose with reasonable accuracy, at any time, the financial position of the company at that time, and

    (c) To enable the directors to ensure that any accounts required to be prepared comply with the requirements of this Act (and, where applicable, of Article 4 of the IAS Regulation).

(3) Accounting records must, in particular, contain:

    (a) Entries from day to day of all sums of money received and expended by the company and the matters in respect of which the receipt and expenditure takes place, and

    (b) A record of the assets and liabilities of the company.

(4) If the company's business involves dealing in goods, the accounting records must contain:

    (a) Statements of stock (inventory) held by the company at the end of each financial year of the company

    (b) All statements of stock-takings from which any statement of stock, as is mentioned in paragraph (a), has been or is to be prepared, and

    (c) Except in the case of goods sold by way of ordinary retail trade, statements of all goods sold and purchased, showing the goods and the buyers and sellers in sufficient detail to enable all these to be identified.

Accounting records for transactions:	
Accounting records for financial position:	
Matters in respect of which the receipt and expenditure takes place:	
Assets and liabilities:	
Statements of stock held by the company:	

Section 388 of the Companies Act 2006 tells a company where and for how long such accounting records should be kept:

- In the case of a **private company (Ltd),** for **three** years from the date on which they are prepared.

- In the case of a **public company (plc),** for **six** years from the date on which they are prepared.

- A company's accounting records must be **kept** at its registered office or such other place as the directors think fit, and must at all times be open to inspection by the company's officers and auditors.

2.2 The need to provide financial statements

Activity 2: Company concerns

Required

Consider the overview of a typical company. Assume that you represent the shareholders only and that the company's directors are separate people. What concerns might you have about them?

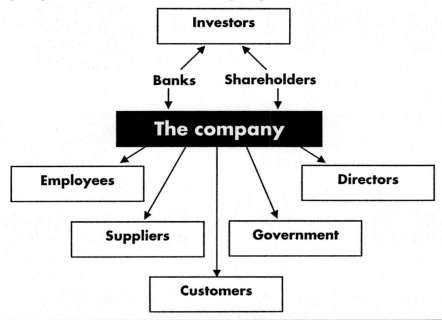

3 The agency problem

You already know from your AAT studies that the Companies Act requires **company accounts** to be produced – the logic of this seems more apparent now. **Forcing** company directors to produce **financial statements** goes some way towards alleviating shareholders' concerns over the **trust** and **visibility** issues raised as part of agency theory.

This is only **half the story**, though – we have seen plenty of examples of companies whose financial statements were misleading to the point of fraud (and beyond, taking **Enron** as a case in point). In some cases, financial statements can be misstated due to **unintentional error**, but what happens if directors attempt to cover their actions by **deliberately falsifying** the company's financial statements?

True and fair view (or presents fairly in all material respects)

'True' can be defined as **honest** and **factual** while 'fair' means **unbiased** and **free from discrimination**. Sometimes, the term 'presents fairly in all material respects' is used instead: this has the same meaning as 'true and fair view' but is often preferred in jurisdictions outside the UK.

The Companies Act puts in a **control** which is designed to **review** the **financial statements** and **supporting disclosures** to conclude with some certainty that directors have been both **honest** and **factual** as well as **unbiased** and **free from discrimination** when reporting the company's position and performance.

This control over financial statements is called the **external audit** and we will spend the rest of this unit looking at how auditors substantiate the terms 'true and fair view' or 'presents fairly in all material respects'.

4 What is an audit?

How does an **audit** address the agency problem? An external audit provides **assurance** to those who need it, which in this case is those stakeholders who rely on the financial statements of a company.

Audit

An audit is an independent review of the financial statements and disclosures produced by directors to ensure that they are both **honest** and **unbiased**.

Assurance

Assurance is a degree of **confidence** that is provided by a practitioner when reviewing subject matter produced by a responsible party for the benefit of the users of that subject matter. Assurance can be expressed in different ways and to different extents.

Illustration 1: Assurance engagements

The following diagram illustrates a typical **assurance engagement**:

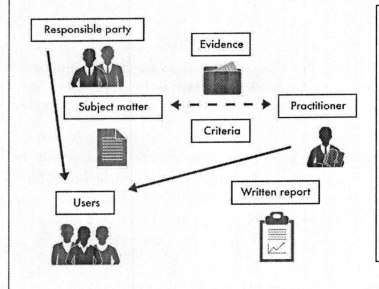

Practical uses of assurance:
- Audits
- Internal control reports
- Reviews of business plans
- Sustainability and corporate social responsibility reports
- Reviews of management performance via KPIs, adherence to voluntary codes etc

Activity 3: Assurance engagements

Assume that the following diagram represents an audit as an example of an assurance engagement – fill in the gaps from the box to describe how the audit would work.

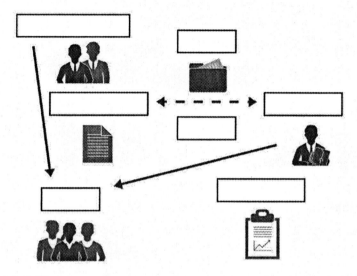

Picklist:

The report = Auditor's report (including their opinion)
The criteria = Auditing, accounting and other standards
The responsible party = Directors
The practitioner = External auditor
The subject matter = Financial statements
The evidence = Outcome of sampling and testing
The users = Shareholders

4.1 Audit appointment

Auditors are usually appointed by shareholders at an Annual General Meeting (AGM) but can be appointed by directors in certain circumstances (such as the date of incorporation, or if the existing auditors resign and replacements need to be appointed before the next AGM). Auditors are usually re-elected annually at the AGM but in private (Ltd) companies that happens automatically unless they are removed by shareholders or they resign (Companies Act 2006: s.485).

4.2 Audit exemptions

While the external audit provides valuable **assurance** to **many stakeholders** and acts as a **deterrent against fraud and error**, as a process it can be **expensive, time consuming** and **inconclusive**. In the event of a company being **owner-managed** (as suggested by the diagram above) the benefit of being provided with an assessment of one's own work can also have limited value.

As a result of these issues, the Companies Act 2006 allows for some companies to be **exempt** from both full reporting and audit requirements, although some information is still required by Companies House.

To qualify for the audit exemption, a company has to satisfy **at least two of the following requirements for two consecutive years**:

- Turnover (revenue) of not more than £10.2 million during the year

- Balance sheet total (statement of financial position) of not more than £5.1 million

- Not more than 50 employees

(Department for Business, Innovation and Skills, 2016)

The audit exemption **cannot** be claimed if a company falls into one of the following:

- A public, or listed, company (plc)

- A bank or insurance company

- A company that is part of a group of companies that are public companies, banks or insurance companies.

Dormant companies (those which have not recorded any transactions within the relevant accounting period) are also exempt from audit provided they are not a bank or insurance company, they are not required to produce group accounts and they fulfil two of the three criteria above. However, they can be a plc (Companies Act 2006, s.477–481).

4.3 Benefits gained from assurance

Despite the cost and disruption associated with the audit, and the fact that owner-managers may feel they have no agency problem to address, many companies that are exempt from audit still choose to have one – why do you think this is?

- There is obvious value from having an independent, qualified accountant **review the business** including its financial records and systems (including the staff it employs and the technology it relies upon).

- It **satisfies external stakeholders** such as banks and shareholders that the business is operating satisfactorily.

- It can act as a **deterrent** against the threat of **fraud** occurring in the business.

- The business may **grow** to levels beyond the exemption threshold one day so getting used to an audit now makes it less difficult to have one in the future.

Now that we know why people have audits, we will look in more detail at what an audit actually is and how it is done, including the various forms of report that can be used to provide the assurance offered by the auditor.

5 ISA 200 *Overall Objectives of the Independent Auditor and the Conduct of an Audit in Accordance with International Standards on Auditing (ISAs)*

An audit helps to provide the required **assurance** via its **report** to shareholders by following a series of **procedures** laid down by auditing standards known as **International Standards on Auditing (ISAs)**. You will need to be familiar with the detail of a number of these ISAs which you will find within this Course Book. The first and perhaps most important one, ISA 200 *Overall Objectives of the Independent Auditor and the Conduct of an Audit in Accordance with International Standards on Auditing*, covers the basics of audit and introduces an amount of useful terminology using the following paragraphs.

'Overall Objectives of the Auditor

In conducting an audit of financial statements, the **overall objectives** of the auditor are:

(a) To obtain reasonable assurance about whether the financial statements as a whole are free from material misstatement, whether due to fraud or error, thereby enabling the auditor to express an opinion on whether the financial statements are prepared, in all material respects, in accordance with an applicable financial reporting framework; and

(b) To report on the financial statements, and communicate as required by the ISAs, in accordance with the auditor's findings.'

(ISA 200: para. 11)

5.1 Regulation

'The purpose of an audit is to **enhance the degree of confidence of intended users** in the financial statements. This is achieved by the expression of an **opinion** by the auditor on whether the financial statements are prepared, in all material respects, in accordance with an **applicable financial reporting framework**. In the case of most general purpose frameworks, that **opinion** is on whether the financial statements are **presented fairly**, in all material respects, or give a **true and fair view** in accordance with the framework. An audit conducted in accordance with ISAs and relevant **ethical requirements** enables the auditor to form that opinion.'

(ISA 200: para. 3)

The opinion that is delivered via the auditor's report will be covered in a later chapter. Such an opinion uses the terms 'true' and 'fair' view (defined earlier) or 'presents fairly in all material respects'.

'Applicable financial reporting framework' refers to the generally accepted accounting principles or GAAP that is in place and which regulates the format of the financial statements. It is the auditor's job to make sure that the financial statements presented are in agreement with this GAAP. The audit will need to be carried out in line with recognised auditing standards (such as ISAs which are produced by the International Auditing and Assurance Standards Board (IAASB) and adopted by the Financial Reporting Council (FRC) in the UK).

The **Financial Reporting Council (FRC)** is the independent regulator of accounting and auditing in the UK. The Government has delegated responsibility for standard-setting to the FRC as well as quality inspections, corporate governance and disciplinary action across the accountancy profession.

The **International Audit and Assurance Standards Board (IAASB)** is an independent body, part of the International Federation of Accountants (IFAC), which sets international standards for auditing.

The ISAs set by the IAASB have been adopted by the UK's FRC as national requirements in the UK. The IAASB is committed to setting high-quality standards for auditing. It also seeks to enable convergence between national and international standards so that globally, the quality of auditing is increased and auditing practice

becomes more uniform around the world. It is thought that this will help ensure public confidence in the audit process (IAASB, 2011).

New standards are researched and consulted on, then subjected to public debate. The resulting draft standards are exposed to the public for comment. Any comments arising are considered and acted upon if necessary. A new standard is then issued when at least two-thirds of the IAASB's members approve it.

The ISAs contain objectives, requirements and application and other explanatory material to help an auditor obtain reasonable assurance. The auditor must follow the requirements of relevant ISAs and must also have an understanding of the whole text of an ISA to enable requirements to be applied properly.

5.2 Responsibilities for producing financial statements

'The financial statements subject to audit are those of the entity, **prepared by management of the entity with oversight from those charged with governance**. ISAs do not impose responsibilities on management or those charged with governance and do not override laws and regulations that govern their responsibilities. However, an audit in accordance with ISAs is conducted on the premise that management and, where appropriate, those charged with governance have acknowledged certain responsibilities that are fundamental to the conduct of the audit. The audit of the financial statements does not relieve management or those charged with governance of their responsibilities.'

(ISA 200: para. 4)

This part of the ISA confirms that there are different parties 'in charge' of a company (the audit client in this case):

- Management prepare the financial statements and are responsible to the board of directors.

- The board of directors is responsible to shareholders (this is known as governance).

Are there any responsibilities that apply to **auditors**? We know that ISAs must be followed by auditors, but **what else** must the auditor consider? Some of this is illustrated by ISA 250 *Consideration of Laws and Regulations in an Audit of Financial Statements* which states that the auditor needs to be aware of the following:

- Laws (such as the UK Companies Act 2006)
- Regulations (such as the UK Corporate Governance Code)
- Case Law (ISA 250: para. A7)

5.3 Professional liability

As we know, the audit is an exercise carried out for the benefit of the shareholders of a company, as it is addressed to them. It enhances the confidence of users to know that the directors have put together financial statements that are free from material misstatement.

If the auditors give a poor service; that is, if they perform an audit that is of substandard quality (for example, which states there are no material misstatements in the financial statements when there are), they may be liable to the shareholders as a result. Performing a poor-quality audit may constitute **negligence** under English law, which is a matter for the courts to decide.

Negligence is the way in which a service is carried out (ie carelessly) and the legal wrong which arises when a person breaks a legal duty of care that is owed to another and causes loss to that other.

For negligence to be proven, three separate things must be established:

(1)   The fact that a duty of care existed
(2)   The fact that this duty of care was breached
(3)   The fact that this caused loss to the claimant

(1)   **Duty of care**

Under English law, auditors owe a duty of care to their client. The **duty of care** is a legal obligation to meet a required standard of care towards another party. This duty is implied into the **contract** between an auditor and a client, and cannot be disputed. Therefore, in negligence cases, if the claimant is the client with whom the audit firm has a contract, point (1) above needs no further proof.

In the case of auditors, this is slightly complicated by the question of who the client is.

We have noted above that the audit is conducted for the benefit of shareholders.

However, in English law, the shareholders of a company are often not considered in isolation; that is, as individuals, but as a single body. In that context, the shareholders are described as being the company.

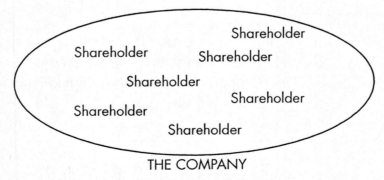

THE COMPANY

It is the **body of shareholders**, known as the company, that is considered to be the client for the purposes of negligence in audit.

When the body of shareholders (the company) as a whole sues for negligence, point (1) above does not have to be proven.

The situation is different if an individual shareholder or another third party sues for negligence.

The audit is primarily carried out for the shareholders. However, other parties may be interested in the financial statements of a company. In most companies, the following parties may be interested.

- The **bank** (often a major lender to the company)

- **Suppliers** (who may extend credit to the company)

- **Customers** (who rely on the company to provide a quality service)

- **Employees** (who rely on the company for income)

- **Tax authorities** (who want to levy the correct tax from the company)

- If the company is public limited, **potential investors** (who are considering whether to invest in the company)

- **Individual investors** (who might want to increase or decrease their stake in a company).

While all of these parties may be interested in the audited financial statements, it is important to remember that the audit is not carried out for their benefit. They are not the client, and **English law has historically substantially restricted the chances of these parties proving the auditors owed them a duty of care**.

One reason for this is that, in the case of these parties, the auditor **does not automatically owe them a duty of care**, and **they would have to prove that one existed**.

The way that a duty of care **might** exist is **if these parties have constructed a relationship with the auditors**, for example by:

- Warning them that they believe a duty of care exists; or

- Telling them they are relying on the audited financial statements for a special purpose.

However, even then, **it is not automatic**, and the auditors may be able to disclaim liability to these parties and say that a duty of care did not exist. Then **the courts will have to decide whether such a duty did exist, examining the facts**.

(2) **Breach of duty of care**

For all parties, not only does a duty of care have to exist, but the claimant must also prove that this **duty was breached**.

Again, this is a matter for the courts to determine when presented with the facts. However, there are some generally accepted principles about auditing which may indicate whether a duty of care has been met or breached.

For example, it is generally accepted that auditors will conduct audits according to professional standards. We discussed this in Chapter 1. You should bear in mind that if an audit firm does not carry out audits according to these professional standards, it may make it easier to prove that a duty of care has been breached by the firm.

(3) **Loss caused**

This is the third item that needs proving in a case of negligence. The claimant will have to show not only that he has suffered a loss, usually a financial loss, but also that the **loss was as a result of the breach of the duty of care on the part of the auditors**. Again, this will be determined by the courts.

If the auditors are found to have been negligent, they may have to pay financial reparation (known as damages) to the claimant.

Activity 4: Duty of care

Select whether the auditors owe a duty of care to the following parties using the drop-down options.

Company	▼
Bank	▼
Individual shareholder	▼
Creditor	▼

Picklist:

Automatic
Must be proved
Never

5.4 Audit failure

Performing a poor-quality audit resulting in the auditors being found guilty of negligence can be described as **audit failure**, which can have serious consequences for audit firms.

One such consequence of audit failure has already been mentioned. A firm may have to pay out substantial damages to a claimant if it has been proven that the auditors were negligent. This would clearly adversely affect the audit firm, and may even cause it to cease to operate, if the damages were so sizeable as to bankrupt the firm.

Such a legal case against a firm would bring substantial bad publicity, impacting on the firm's ability to retain and engage clients in the future, even if they did continue to operate.

In addition, audit firms have supervisory bodies that monitor their activities (in the UK, that is the FRC). The FRC might take disciplinary action against the firm and its partners in the event of negligence, which could result in its ability to conduct audits being suspended.

5.5 Restriction of liability

The Companies Act 2006 entitles auditors to negotiate **liability limitation agreements** with their clients. The effect of such agreements is to restrict the extent of the auditors' liability (the amount of damages to be paid) in the event that negligence is proved against them. This restriction may be a specified amount above which an auditor will not be liable (a **liability cap**) or an agreement that, if there are other parties contributing to the loss and the damage, the auditor will only be held liable for his portion of the damage (**proportional liability**) (Companies Act 2006: s.534).

There are other ways that auditors can restrict their liability. Many firms include a statement in their auditor's report specifically excluding liability to parties other than the shareholders. This is known as a Bannerman paragraph, after the legal case in which such a course of action was recommended for auditors to avoid liability to third parties.

Individual audit partners can limit their personal liability for the firm's debts from such matters by changing how the audit firm is legally formed.

Traditionally, audit firms have been partnerships, where each partner is liable for the debts of the firm jointly with the other partners. It is now possible to set up audit firms in different legal forms, such as a limited liability partnership (LLP), where the partners have limited liability in the same way that shareholders in a company do. There are some drawbacks to forming an LLP, however: for example, the requirements for increased publicity, such as filing accounts with the Companies Registrar.

Lastly, a firm may insure against professional liability by taking out professional indemnity insurance. In fact, many audit firms are required to do this by their supervisory body in the public interest, so that if a firm is found liable, the injured parties can be compensated.

5.6 Reasonable assurance

'As the basis for the auditor's opinion, ISAs require the auditor to obtain **reasonable assurance** about whether the financial statements as a whole are free from **material misstatement**, whether due to **fraud** or **error**. Reasonable assurance is a high level of assurance. It is obtained when the auditor has obtained **sufficient appropriate audit evidence** to **reduce audit risk** (that is, the risk that the auditor expresses an inappropriate opinion when the financial statements are materially misstated) to an **acceptably low level**. However, reasonable assurance is **not an absolute level of assurance**, because there are **inherent limitations** of an audit which result in most of the audit evidence on which the auditor draws conclusions and bases the auditor's opinion being **persuasive** rather than **conclusive**.'

(ISA 200: para. 5)

Notice this is only reasonable assurance and is later confirmed as not being absolute due to limitations. It is therefore not realistic to expect that an audit will pick up all issues, only those judged as material from the evidence collected (which is usually only a sample taken from the relevant population).

This gives some explanation of why the auditor delivers an **opinion** only and **not** a **guarantee**. In paragraph 6 of ISA 200 you will see that the auditor relies heavily on informed judgement.

Note the distinction between fraud and error – one of the inherent limitations that the ISA describes.

Activity 5: Types and levels of assurance

Required

Identify whether the following sentences display a type of assurance or an expression of assurance and, for each one, select the most appropriate description from the picklist below:

'In our opinion, the financial statements present fairly, in all material respects...'	▼
This is provided as part of the auditor's opinion and is classed as high, but not absolute.	▼
This is not provided for an audit as it is only moderate and is insufficient for an audit.	▼
'Based on our review, nothing has come to our attention that causes us to believe that the financial statements are presented unfairly, in all material respects...'	▼

Picklist:

Limited assurance
Negative expression of assurance
Positive expression of assurance
Reasonable assurance

5.7 Fraud issues from management and other employees

As stated above, an audit is not designed to uncover fraud. ISA 240 *The Auditor's Responsibilities Relating to Fraud in an Audit of Financial Statements* states that primary responsibility for preventing and detecting fraud rests with those charged with the governance of an entity, and management (ISA 240: para. 4). When we look at a company's control environment later in this course, we will see it is primarily through internal controls that a company tries to prevent fraud.

An auditor is still responsible for detecting material misstatements which may have arisen due to fraud. The inherent limitations discussed above are particularly significant in relation to a fraud which people are attempting to hide. It may be even more difficult to detect management fraud than employee fraud because management may be able to manipulate financial records themselves. It is therefore very important for auditors to have 'professional scepticism', and to be alert to identifying opportunities for fraud to take place.

Professional scepticism is the attitude of critical assessment and the use of a questioning mind necessary to prevent overlooking suspicious circumstances or from drawing incorrect conclusions. The auditor should neither assume that management is dishonest nor fail to question whether they are honest.

Activity 6: Fraud and error

Required

What do you think is the main difference between fraud and error?

Why will this make fraud more of an issue to auditors than error?

Many of the ISAs in existence use the term '**professional scepticism**' on numerous occasions to alert the auditor to the dangers of placing unrealistic levels of **trust** in both the management and other staff employed by the entity being audited. To combat this, the Companies Act 2006 (s.507) states that if an employee of the company knowingly or recklessly gives the auditors a false or deceptive statement they are guilty of a criminal offence.

From the **inherent limitations of internal controls** to the **risks associated with giving an audit opinion**, this seems more and more likely to revolve around not just errors but also **fraud**, so auditors need to remember that the risk of material misstatement through fraud is increased when the auditor is sceptical of management's **attitude** and/or **integrity**.

The term '**money laundering**' covers most aspects of fraud, including the following:

- Offences that indicate dishonest behaviour – such as tax evasion or not returning overpayments by customers (where the client has attempted but failed to return such overpayments, dishonesty is not indicated)

- Offences that involve saved costs (such as where a company is saving money by not complying with environmental law; for example, by dumping waste illegally rather than paying a company to remove it)

- Conduct overseas that would be illegal in the UK – for example, bribery of government officials

The **Proceeds of Crime Act 2002** sets down responsibilities for auditors to inform the **National Crime Agency (NCA)** of any suspicions they may have regarding money laundering – they must not alert the suspect, though, as 'tipping off' is classified as a crime as well (Proceeds of Crime Act 2002, s.333).

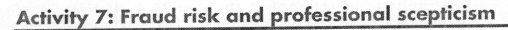

Activity 7: Fraud risk and professional scepticism

Required

Identify whether each of the following factors would be likely to cause the auditor a greater or lesser degree of professional scepticism by selecting the appropriate option.

	Greater professional scepticism?	Lesser professional scepticism?
The finance director has requested that you complete the audit on time in order to meet head office reporting deadlines. The finance director has a profit-related bonus but has always accepted adjustments that you asked for on previous audits.		
The payroll officer has asked that you do not perform any testing of the payroll until she returns from her holiday. There are no other members of staff who can assist you with the payroll audit.		
When reviewing the board minutes, you read that the company has applied for significant funding to support the currently poor cash flow. From recent conversations with the chief accountant, however, you were under the impression that revenue and cash flow were both healthy and that the company was performing well.		

5.8 Professional judgement

'The concept of **materiality** is applied by the auditor both in planning and performing the audit, and in evaluating the effect of identified misstatements on the audit and of uncorrected misstatements, if any, on the financial statements. In general, misstatements, including omissions, are **considered to be material if, individually or in the aggregate, they could reasonably be expected to influence the economic decisions of users taken on the basis of the financial statements**. Judgments about materiality are made in the light of surrounding circumstances, and are affected by the **auditor's perception of the financial information needs of users of the financial statements**, and by the **size** or **nature** of a misstatement, or a combination of both. The auditor's opinion deals with the financial statements as a whole and therefore the auditor is not responsible for the detection of misstatements that are not material to the financial statements as a whole.'

(ISA 200: para. 6)

Materiality is the measure by which the auditor decides whether something needs investigating further or not.

The **perception** of the auditor must be extremely clear to ensure that items are not ignored – otherwise, the implications for the auditor (summed up by the phrase 'audit risk' used earlier) could be severe.

Such judgement in the light of applicable laws and regulations (as well as the ISAs) dictate the approach that the auditor uses.

5.9 Evidence

'The ISAs contain objectives, requirements and application and other explanatory material that are designed to support the auditor in obtaining reasonable assurance. The ISAs require that the auditor exercise **professional judgment** and maintain **professional scepticism** throughout the planning and performance of the audit and, among other things:

- Identify and assess risks of material misstatement, whether due to fraud or error, based on an **understanding of the entity** and its environment, including the entity's internal control.

- Obtain **sufficient appropriate audit evidence** about whether material misstatements exist, through designing and implementing appropriate responses to the assessed risks.

- **Form an opinion** on the financial statements based on **conclusions** drawn from the audit evidence obtained.'

(ISA 200: para. 7)

The terms **'scepticism'** and **'judgement'** appear again to reinforce the alertness required by the auditor.

We will see more of the need to **understand the entity** later in the course.

Obtaining evidence is how the auditor reaches a conclusion and forms an opinion — we will also look at ways of obtaining evidence. The Companies Act 2006 assists auditors by giving them a right of access at all times to all the company's books, accounts and vouchers and to require all company officers to supply whatever information and explanation they feel is necessary for the audit.

Scepticism includes learning to tell **when things may not be as they appear**, even when **interviewing clients** and **documenting** such discussions.

5.10 Reporting

'The form of opinion expressed by the auditor will depend upon the applicable financial reporting framework and any applicable **law** or regulation.'

(ISA 200: para. 8)

The auditor's report varies by jurisdiction depending on where the audit is taking place.

The auditor's report contains a number of elements that you will learn more about later in this unit, but in summary it looks like this:

- A title and a suitable addressee

- The auditor's opinion and an explanation of the basis for that opinion including a description of the scope of the audit

- Issues related to the audited entity's going concern, key audit matters from the audit and other information (these are not all required for every audit, though)

- Responsibilities of both auditors and management for the financial statements

- Regulatory issues for the jurisdiction concerned

- The auditor's signature, address and date that the report was signed (ISA 700: Appendix).

'The auditor may also have certain other communication and reporting responsibilities to users, management, **those charged with governance**, or **parties outside the entity**, in relation to matters arising from the audit. These may be **established** by the ISAs or **by applicable law** or regulation. (ISA 200: para. 9)

Effective Date

This ISA is effective for audits of financial statements for periods beginning on or after December 15, 2009.'

(ISA 200: para. 10)

Auditors face a tricky balancing act in recognising the importance of **confidential information** obtained during the course of the audit and the need to report any instances of **money laundering** that they may uncover at any time.

Auditors should be informed of the date of any shareholder meetings and allowed to attend and speak about matters relevant to the audit.

'In all cases when reasonable assurance cannot be obtained and a **qualified opinion** in the auditor's report is insufficient in the circumstances for purposes of reporting to the intended users of the financial statements, the ISAs require that the auditor **disclaim** an opinion or **withdraw** (or resign) from the engagement, where withdrawal is possible under applicable law or regulation.'

(ISA 200: para. 12)

In cases where the auditor cannot simply give a 'true and fair' opinion, there may be cases where a different opinion is given – one **qualified** by a statement such as '...*except for ... the financial statements show a true and fair view...*' Again, we will see more of this in a later part of the Course Book.

6 The AAT Code of Professional Ethics

The assurance sought by the intended users could be **compromised** by the external auditor not being **fully independent** from the directors of the company being audited. The audit profession has addressed this issue by creating a number of **ethical principles** that should underpin all audit work with concepts such as **independence** and **objectivity** as well as **recommended courses of action** should any member find themselves exposed, and these can be found within the AAT Code of Professional Ethics (2014). This Code is made available on the AAT website (www.aat.org.uk) and AAT members are required to act in accordance with the Code. You should have already met and studied the Code in earlier units.

Independence is defined by the Code in two ways:

(i) **Independence of mind** – Independence of mind is the state of mind that permits the provision of an opinion without being affected by influences that compromise professional judgement, allowing an individual to act with integrity, and exercise objectivity and professional judgement; and

(ii) **Independence in appearance** – Independence in appearance is the avoidance of facts and circumstances that are so significant that a reasonable and informed third party, having knowledge of all relevant information, including any safeguards applied, would reasonably conclude a firm's, or a member of the assurance team's, integrity, objectivity or professional scepticism had been compromised.

(AAT Code of Professional Ethics: s.290.5)

6.1 Fundamental principles

These are the ethical principles that all accountants and auditors should comply with.

To help understand how this independence can be displayed, there are a series of **fundamental principles** that should be complied with:

- **Professional competence and due care**: to maintain professional knowledge and skill at the level required to ensure that a client or employer receives competent professional service based on current developments in practice, legislation and techniques. A member shall act diligently and in accordance with applicable technical and professional standards when providing professional services.

- **Integrity**: to be straightforward and honest in all professional and business relationships.

- **Adopt Professional behaviour**: to comply with relevant laws and regulations and avoid any action that brings our profession into disrepute.

- **Confidentiality**: to, in accordance with the law, respect the confidentiality of information acquired as a result of professional and business relationships and not disclose any such information to third parties without proper and specific authority unless there is a legal or professional right or duty to disclose. Confidential information acquired as a result of professional and business relationships shall not be used for the personal advantage of the member or third parties (we will return to this in different situations later).

- **Objectivity**: to not allow bias, conflict of interest or undue influence of others to override professional or business judgements.

(AAT Code of Professional Ethics: s.100.5)

You can remember these more easily with the mnemonic '**PIPCO**'.

Activity 8: Fundamental ethical principles

Required

Match each of the following descriptions with the fundamental ethical principle it represents.

Being dishonest about a business relationship with a client		▼
Accepting an engagement when not trained to complete it		▼
Insider trading by deciding to purchase a client's shares		▼

Picklist:

Confidentiality
Integrity
Objectivity
Professional behaviour
Professional competence and due care

6.2 The conceptual framework

These are potential situations or ethical threats that auditors and accountants should aim to avoid.

In order to help auditors **avoid** getting into situations where their independence or objectivity could be called into question, the Code uses the **conceptual framework** to illustrate the possible threats that auditors could be exposed to:

- **Advocacy**: when a member promotes a position or opinion to the point that subsequent objectivity may be compromised

- **Self-interest**: where a financial or other interest will inappropriately influence the member's judgement or behaviour

- **Intimidation**: when a member may be deterred from acting objectively by threats, whether actual or perceived

- **Familiarity**: when, because of a close or personal relationship, a member becomes too sympathetic to the interests of others

- **Self-review**: when a previous judgement needs to be re-evaluated by the member responsible for that judgement

(AAT Code of Professional Ethics: s.100.12)

You can remember these more easily by the mnemonic '**AS IFS**'.

There are actually **many circumstances** that threaten the application of the fundamental principles and we will now have a look at each of these threats to see just what can lead to them appearing.

Illustration 2: Application of the fundamental principles

Advocacy

- Promoting shares in a listed entity when that entity is a financial statement audit client

- Acting as an advocate on behalf of an assurance client in litigation or disputes with third parties

Self-interest

- A financial interest in a client or jointly holding a financial interest with a client

- Undue dependence on total fees from a client

- Having a close business relationship with a client

- Concern about the possibility of losing a client

- Potential employment with a client

- Contingent fees relating to an assurance engagement

- A loan to or from an assurance client or any of its directors or officers

- Discovering a significant error when evaluating the results of a previous professional service performed by a member of staff working with or for the member

Intimidation

- Being threatened with dismissal or replacement in relation to a client engagement

- An assurance client indicating that he will not award a planned non-assurance contract to the member in practice if the member in practice continues to disagree with the client's accounting treatment for a particular transaction

- Being threatened with litigation

- Being pressured to reduce inappropriately the quality or extent of work performed in order to reduce fees

- Feeling pressured to agree with the judgement of a client employee because the employee has more expertise on the matter in question

Familiarity

- A member of the engagement team having a close or personal relationship with a director or officer of the client

- A member of the engagement team having a close or personal relationship with an employee of the client who is in a position to exert direct and significant influence over the subject matter of the engagement

- A former partner of the firm being a director or officer of the client or an employee in a position to exert direct and significant influence over the subject matter of the engagement

- Accepting gifts or preferential treatment from a client, unless the value is clearly insignificant

- Long association of senior personnel with the assurance client

Self-review

- The discovery of a significant error during a re-evaluation of the work of the member in practice

- Reporting on the operation of financial systems after being involved in their design or implementation

- Having prepared the original data used to generate records that are the subject matter of the engagement

- A member of the assurance team being, or having recently been, a director or officer of that client

- A member of the assurance team being, or having recently been, employed by the client in a position to exert significant influence over the subject matter of the engagement

- Performing a service for a client that directly affects the subject matter of the assurance engagement

Activity 9: Ethical threats

Required

Which ONE of the following situations is likely to represent a self-interest threat?

	✓
One client represents 25% of the audit firm's total fees for the year	
Representing an audit client in a tax investigation	
Receiving free VIP tickets to the World Cup Final from a client	

6.3 Members in practice

There are certain situations where accountants and auditors who work in practice may be exposed to ethical threats which we shall now discuss.

- **Professional appointment** – before accepting an engagement to work for a client, members should determine whether there are threats to compliance with the fundamental principles from any illegal activities (such as money laundering), dishonesty on the part of clients or questionable financial reporting practices. Members should also ensure they are competent to act before accepting a professional appointment (AAT Code of Professional Ethics: s.210).

- **Second opinions** – if asked to provide a second opinion on the application of accounting, auditing, reporting or any other standards or principles to an entity that is not an existing client, members need to ensure they are competent to act in such a capacity and have access to the same relevant facts or evidence as the existing accountant. Members need to be alert to second opinions being abused by clients especially if they are not permitted to communicate with the existing accountant (AAT Code of Professional Ethics: s.230).

- **Fees and other types of remuneration** – members may quote whatever fee they feel is appropriate for a service but they must be alert to any threats presented by fees being too low (such as self-interest if the fee quoted to clients is so low that it may be difficult to perform the engagement in line with applicable technical and professional standards). Arrangements such as contingent fees and commissions can also present self-interest threats depending on the engagement and which, without adequate safeguards, are unacceptable (AAT Code of Professional Ethics: s.240).

- **Marketing professional services** – like all service providers, accountants need to advertise to attract clients but they must ensure that they do so in a manner that does not distort the truth or misrepresent the interests of another professional: otherwise, a self-interest threat to compliance with the principle of professional behaviour may be created (AAT Code of Professional Ethics: s.250).

- **Gifts and hospitality** – it is not uncommon for members and their clients to give and receive items as part of maintaining their professional relationship. However, such gifts and hospitality may create self-interest threats if accepted and intimidation threats if made public. In such cases, the significance of any gifts and hospitality must always be considered, especially in the context of the UK Bribery Act 2010 (AAT Code of Professional Ethics: s.260).

- **Custody of client assets** – members may be asked to look after client assets (such as cash or valuables) due to possessing better safekeeping controls, but this could create self-interest threats and others relating to money laundering that they should consider before accepting this request (AAT Code of Professional Ethics: s.270).

- **Objectivity – all services** – threats such as familiarity can be created by having a close personal or business relationship with a client or its directors, officers or the employees of a client (AAT Code of Professional Ethics: s.280).

- **Independence – assurance engagements** – family and other personal or business relationships, loans, beneficial interests in shares and other investments and gifts and hospitality can create threats to objectivity and independence by their nature. Members should evaluate the threats and use professional judgement in applying the conceptual framework in such cases (AAT Code of Professional Ethics: s.290).

6.4 Members in business

Members in business may be solely or jointly responsible for the preparation and reporting of financial and other information, which both their employing organisations and third parties may rely on. They may also be responsible for providing effective financial management and competent advice on a variety of business-related matters.

A member in business may be, for example, a salaried employee, a partner, a director (whether executive or non-executive), an owner-manager, a volunteer or another working for one or more employing organisations.

A member in business has a responsibility to further the legitimate aims of their employing organisation. The Code seeks not to hinder a member in business from properly fulfilling that responsibility but to consider circumstances in which conflicts may be created with the duty to comply with the fundamental principles.

As well as being exposed to the same ethical threats as members working in practice, members in business may experience the following:

- **Self-interest threats** from inappropriate personal use of corporate assets, concern over employment security and commercial pressure from outside their employer (self-interest threats also occur when members in business are exposed to profit-related bonuses and share options when in a position to influence the factors that could affect such schemes).

- **Self-review threats** when reviewing data and making decisions based on the same data.

- **Advocacy threats** would only exist for a member in business who promotes their employing organisation if any statements made were either false or misleading.

- **Familiarity threats** exist where reporting is undertaken by members and those connected to members, where there is long association with business contacts and where gifts are given and/or received.

- **Intimidation** can occur when a member is threatened with either dismissal or replacement while producing some form of subject matter or when a dominant individual attempts to influence decisions.

- A threat to the member in business performing duties with the appropriate degree of **professional competence and due care** due to insufficient time, resource, training or information being provided by the employer.

- **Gifts and hospitality** can be perceived to act as inducements which create both self-interest and intimidation threats as outlined above.

6.5 Ethical safeguards

As part of the assessment, you will need to be able to evaluate **ethical safeguards**.

Ethical safeguards either eliminate or reduce threats to objectivity and independence.

They can be considered like this:

Illustration 3: Ethical safeguards

Firm-wide safeguards to eliminate or reduce threats to the fundamental ethical principles and the independence of auditors:	
The use of different personnel with different reporting lines for the provision of non-assurance services to an audited entity	Necessary for the following engagements to address the likely self-review, self-interest and advocacy threats: • Internal audit services • Information technology services • Valuation services (including actuarial services) • Tax services • Litigation support and legal services • Recruitment and remuneration services • Corporate finance services • Transaction related services • Restructuring services • Accounting services
Procedures for monitoring and managing the reliance on revenue received from a single client	Self-interest and intimidation threats can be mitigated by: • Reducing the dependency on the client • External quality control reviews • Consulting a third party on key points.
Procedures that will enable the identification of interests or relationships between the firm or members of the engagement team and clients	Examples of relevant interests or relationships (plus relevant safeguards where appropriate): • Financial interests (self-interest, familiarity and intimidation threats can be reduced by a variety of safeguards, usually removal of either the interest or the individual concerned, or review) • Loans and guarantees (create a self-interest threat that is insurmountable unless under normal commercial terms) • Business relationships (create self-interest and intimidation threats that are usually insurmountable unless such transactions are part of normal business and at arm's length) • Personal and family relationships (create self-interest, familiarity and intimidation threats that can usually only be addressed by removing the affected individual from the engagement team)

	• Switching jobs between engagement firms and the client (self-interest, self-review, familiarity and intimidation threats may be created which are so significant that no safeguard could reduce the threat to an acceptable level – however, if appropriate, safeguards can include modifying work plans, appointing experienced staff and review procedures)
	• Serving as a director or officer of an assurance client (self-review, self-interest and advocacy threats here are usually insurmountable unless the service is limited to matters of a routine and administrative nature only)
	• Gifts and hospitality (self-interest and familiarity threats are created that are insurmountable unless the value is trivial and inconsequential)
	• Actual or threatened litigation (self-interest and intimidation threats can be mitigated by withdrawal or review).
	In most instances, such procedures will require communicating any interests or relationships to those charged with governance at the client and documenting the nature of any threats and any conclusions on the adequacy of safeguards adopted (where appropriate).
	This can include being alert to interests or relationships between the firm or members of the engagement team and related entities of the client.
Disciplinary mechanisms to promote compliance with policies and procedures	These will be implemented by firms to ensure adherence to the AAT Code of Ethics (and to punish those who do not follow these policies and procedures).

Engagement-specific safeguards to eliminate or reduce threats to the fundamental ethical principles and the independence of auditors:

Independent review of audit working papers	As above, many situations can lead to the need for an independent review of someone's work: • Financial interests • Employment switches between firms and clients • Litigation threats. Also necessary in cases where staff require rotating due to the length of their association with a particular client (see below).

Consultation with an independent third party	Necessary in such cases as excessive fee dependence on one specific client (and with AAT in cases of ethical uncertainty).
Disclosure and discussion of ethical issues with those charged with governance	Usually required in cases where interests and relationships exist between the firm or members of the engagement team and clients.
Rotation of senior personnel	Long association between engagement staff and clients can lead to familiarity and self-interest threats – depending on the significance of the threat, rotation away from the engagement team is an appropriate safeguard to counter this threat, as is a review of the staff member's work by a professional accountant not on the team and regular independent internal and external quality review.

Matters that should be referred to senior members of audit staff:

These are frequently subjective and require staff members to display suitable judgement (these will be covered in a subsequent part of the Course Book).

(AAT Code of Professional Ethics: s.300)

Activity 10: Ethical safeguards

Required

For each of the following situations, match the ethical threat described with an appropriate safeguard.

Providing a valuation service to an audit client for assets held by a subsidiary of that client.	
Seven members of the audit firm own shares in the firm's audit clients.	▼
The audit manager's brother is promoted to become finance director of that client.	▼

Picklist:

A register of interests and relationships between audit team members and clients
Independent review of working papers
Rotation of senior personnel
Use of different personnel with different reporting lines

6.6 Confidentiality

We've already seen that members are obliged to maintain **confidentiality** of information acquired as a result of professional and business relationships, but are there situations where this may not be appropriate? The Code provides details of three such cases:

(1)   Where disclosure is **permitted** by law and is authorised by the client or the employer (or any other person to whom an obligation of confidence is owed) such as prospective auditors asking a client's permission to contact their existing auditor.

(2)   Where disclosure is **required** by law such as in a court case or if required as part of an investigation by HM Revenue & Customs (HMRC) or the NCA in relation to money laundering (in such cases, though, great care must be taken by auditors to avoid 'tipping off' those under suspicion as this represents a crime in itself).

(3)   Where there is a **professional duty** or right to disclose, which is in the **public interest**, and is not prohibited by law (this may occur as part of an external quality review or as part of a regulatory body's inquiry or inspection, and is usually to assist the member in protecting their own professional interests).

Accountants are unlikely to breach the fundamental principle of confidentiality lightly so legal and other professional advice is always advised in such situations (AAT Code of Professional Ethics: s.140).

Security

In practice, security measures by the auditor may be a very important part of keeping the duty of confidentiality. Security falls into two categories.

First, auditors must be very careful in carrying out their work that they do not discuss their work in inappropriate places. This may be the case both at the client and outside the client's premises.

For example, the directors may tell the auditors information that they don't want the rest of the client staff to know. The auditors should only discuss such information when they know other client staff members cannot overhear them.

For this reason, it is very important that the client provides the auditors with a suitable place to work when they are carrying out auditing work at a client's premises. They should be given a private room rather than being asked to work in the middle of the accounts department.

The auditors must be careful in discussing client information away from the client premises.

There are many places where it is inappropriate to discuss client information. The general rule is that client information should not be discussed in a public place or with anyone outside of the audit firm.

Second, auditors must ensure that the security arrangements over their physical work are sufficient. Audit files and any computers storing audit work must be kept secure. Auditors are often issued with lockable cases by their firm so that they can lock audit files away when they are not in use and can be transported securely.

This may also mean not leaving the office (which the auditors are using at the client) open if the auditors are not there, not leaving client files in the auditor's car, and ensuring that the storage facilities for client files at the auditor's own office are secure. If older files are put away in storage, this should be locked, with only the auditors having access to it.

6.7 Conflicts of interest

Conflicts of interest occur either when a member provides the same service to two competing clients or employers, or the interests of a member in relation to a service are in conflict with the interests of a client or employer due to the same service. This can happen in situations when acting for both parties who are competing for the same contract or assets, and when one party intends to acquire the other (including the firm) and requires evaluation of the relative significance of such conflicts.

Once such a conflict of interest has been identified, members are required to disclose the nature of the conflict and to obtain consent to act from all parties concerned. Without consent, the service cannot be continued or accepted unless the process of obtaining consent represents a breach of confidentiality (such as cases of fraud or hostile takeovers) when safeguards must be in place (usually those relating to preserving confidentiality using information barriers between the different teams working on each client or employer) (AAT Code of Professional Ethics: s.220).

Activity 11: Confidentiality

Required

For each of the following situations, tick any where the auditor is authorised to disclose confidential information about an audit client.

	✓
A request for information as part of a tax investigation	
A change in external auditor following a tender without client approval	
A quality control review carried out by the FRC	

6.8 Conclusions

The overall aim is for external auditors to ensure that the **relationship** they find themselves in **with audit clients** should only ever be that of **'auditor'** and **'client'**. Should a member find that they have failed to comply with any of this, the Code (2014) states:

'Members should note that **disciplinary action** may be taken for **non-compliance** with this Code where the member's conduct is considered to prejudice their status as a member or to reflect adversely on the reputation of AAT.'

Such disciplinary action could result in suspension of membership and possibly even a fine.

Chapter summary

- Companies are legal entities that are set up for a specific purpose and have many different stakeholders (investors such as banks and shareholders, plus employees and directors, customers and suppliers and the Government which is interested in keeping all parties happy!).

- Companies have many responsibilities: in the UK they are laid out by the Companies Act 2006 which specifies two areas for this unit: (i) keeping adequate accounting records and (ii) providing financial statements.

- Due to the differences between owners and directors of a company, there can be a lack of visibility and trust over the truth and fairness of the company's financial statements, which leads to something called the agency problem: this can be overcome by the financial statements being subject to an independent review which is known as an audit.

- Audits are carried out by qualified professionals who are appointed to provide a degree of credibility for the work done by directors in running the company on behalf of the investors who own it. This credibility is called 'assurance'. Not all companies require an audit but there can be benefits from having one voluntarily.

- International Standard on Auditing (ISA) 200 provides a framework for audits carried out using the standards agreed by most accountants and auditors across the world – these are created by the International Auditing and Assurance Standards Board (IAASB) and in the UK are adopted and regulated by the Financial Reporting Council (FRC).

- Many responsibilities exist for both managers and auditors of companies subject to audit – included in these are an awareness of what happens when an audit fails due to auditor negligence and the techniques used by auditors to control such failures.

- Auditors are expected to collect enough evidence during the audit to be able to provide an appropriate amount of assurance for their opinion. Part of this evidence gathering requires auditors to be alert to the threat of fraud such as money laundering: to combat this and other frauds, auditors are encouraged to display 'professional scepticism' in order to apply their judgement appropriately.

- The auditor will communicate the findings of the audit to a variety of stakeholders, including shareholders, those charged with the governance of an entity and regulators, and will do so in a specific manner using an auditor's report.

- To assist auditors and accountants in discharging their duties with the public interest in mind, the AAT Code of Professional Ethics exists to provide guidance on objectivity and independence (both of mind and in appearance). Through the fundamental principles (PIPCO) and the conceptual framework (AS IFS) accountants and auditors both in practice and in business are given guidance that they can apply when necessary, including ethical safeguards to counter various threats plus advice on issues regarding confidentiality and conflicts of interest between competing clients.

- **Assurance:** a degree of **confidence** that is provided by a practitioner when reviewing subject matter produced by a responsible party for the benefit of the users of that subject matter. Assurance can be expressed in different ways and to different extents

- **Audit:** an independent review of the financial statements and disclosures produced by directors to ensure that they are both **honest** and **unbiased**

- **Audit failure:** performing a poor-quality audit resulting in the auditors being found guilty of negligence can be described as audit failure, which can have serious consequences for audit firms

- **Conceptual framework:** potential situations or ethical threats that auditors and accountants should aim to avoid

- **Conflicts of interest:** occur either when a member provides the same service to two competing clients or employers, or the interests of a member in relation to a service are in conflict with the interests of a client or employer due to the same service

- **Ethical safeguards:** either eliminate or reduce threats to objectivity and independence

- **Financial Reporting Council (FRC):** the independent regulator of accounting and auditing in the UK. The Government has delegated responsibility for standard-setting to the FRC as well as quality inspections, corporate governance and disciplinary action across the accountancy profession

- **Fundamental principles:** ethical principles that all accountants and auditors should comply with

- **Independence in appearance:** the avoidance of facts and circumstances that are so significant that a reasonable and informed third party, having knowledge of all relevant information, including any safeguards applied, would reasonably conclude a firm's, or a member of the assurance team's, integrity, objectivity or professional scepticism had been compromised

- **Independence of mind:** the state of mind that permits the provision of an opinion without being affected by influences that compromise professional judgement, allowing an individual to act with integrity, and exercise objectivity and professional judgement

- **International Audit and Assurance Standards Board (IAASB):** an independent body, part of the International Federation of Accountants (IFAC), which sets international standards for auditing

- **Liability limitation agreement**: an agreement between an auditor and their client that limits the amount of auditor liability in the event of any negligence

- **Negligence:** the way in which a service is carried out (ie carelessly) and to the legal wrong which arises when a person breaks a legal duty of care that is owed to another and causes loss to that other It is a key part of determining professional liability

- **Professional scepticism:** the attitude of critical assessment and the use of a questioning mind necessary to challenge assumptions and prevent overlooking suspicious circumstances or from drawing incorrect conclusions

- **Proportional liability**: where a professional firm agrees to be liable for only a share of any damages due to a client on respect of negligence or other litigation

- **True and fair view (or presents fairly in all material respects)**: 'true' means honest and factual, while 'fair' means free from bias. 'Presents fairly in all material respects' is used in the same way as 'true and fair view'

1   Complete the following statement.

A(n) [____ ▼] is a(n) [____ ▼] registered as such under the Companies Act 2006.

Picklist for line items:

Company
Entity

2   Select which one of the following statements is not an implication of registering a company by ticking the appropriate box.

It is seen as distinct from its owners.   ☐

It is required to have an audit, unless exempt.   ☐

It must keep accounting records.   ☐

It must be managed by its owners.   ☐

3   State whether the following are true or false in respect of a company's accounting records.

Companies must keep records that disclose with reasonable accuracy the company's position at any time.	▼
All companies must keep records of inventory.	▼

Picklist:

True
False

4   Complete the following definition of an audit.

A(n) [____ ▼] is an exercise carried out by [____ ▼] to ascertain whether the [____ ▼] prepared by the [____ ▼] are (in the UK) in accordance with UK GAAP and the [____ ▼] and give what is known as a(n) [____ ▼] .

Picklist for line items:

Audit
Auditors
Companies Act 2006
Directors
Financial statements
True and fair view

5   State whether the following statements are true or false in respect of external auditors' duties and rights.

Auditors are required to report on the truth and fairness of financial statements.	▼
Auditors have a right of access to a company's books and records at any time.	▼
Auditors are entitled to obtain explanations from the officers of a company.	▼

Picklist:

True
False

6   Select which one of the following best describes to whom the auditors owe a duty of care by ticking the appropriate box.
Auditors owe a duty of care to:

All users of financial statements ☐

The client (that is, the company, comprising all the shareholders) ☐

Shareholders ☐

The client and any other parties with whom they have
implied a special relationship ☐

7   Set out what three things need to be proven in a case for negligence.

8   Complete the following definition of confidentiality.

[▼] is the duty to keep [▼] affairs [▼]

Picklist for line items:

Client
Confidentiality
Private

9   Set out why security procedures are important to auditors.

10 During the audit of Sneaky Ltd, the audit senior discovered a file of invoices which did not appear to be included in the financial records, for which the company has been paid in cash. No VAT has been paid in relation to these sales.

Select which one of the following is the most appropriate action for the audit senior to take by ticking the appropriate box.

Report the matter to:

The board of directors ☐

HMRC ☐

The audit firm's money laundering reporting officer ☐

All of the above ☐

Systems of
internal control

2

Learning outcomes

3.1	Demonstrate an understanding of the principles of internal control
	• Definition of internal control and each of its components (control environment, control activities, including performance reviews, information processing, physical controls, segregation of duties and monitoring of controls by management and/or an internal audit function)
	• Preventative and detective controls
	• Limitations of internal controls
	• Factors relating to the operating environment and internal control system that influence control risk.
3.2	Identify the main features of an accounting system
	• Control objectives
	• Risks
	• Control procedures for the major accounting systems (purchases, revenue, payroll, inventory, non-current assets, cash and bank).
3.3	Evaluate the effectiveness of an accounting control system
	• Use systems records (flowcharts, internal control questions and checklists) to evaluate internal control systems
	• Use the evaluation of internal controls to determine the audit strategy
	• Identify the merits and limitations of using standardised questionnaires and checklists
	• Identify the factors that contribute to strengths and deficiencies in accounting systems.
3.4	Identify how internal controls mitigate risks
	• Identify the types of errors and irregularities that can occur in accounting systems
	• Identify how errors and irregularities can be prevented or detected by control procedures.

Assessment context

This is a key area in the syllabus and you should expect to see four tasks in your assessment testing this.

Qualification context

This topic includes terminology that you will have seen before in your AAT studies – you should be able to apply this knowledge to address the practical aspects of some of the systems and controls addressed.

Business context

Failure to record a company's controls is a critical issue for auditors; hence the importance that is placed upon it in real audits. You will also see how companies are structured to ensure such critical systems work to keep track of the many transactions undertaken on a daily (even hourly) basis.

Chapter overview

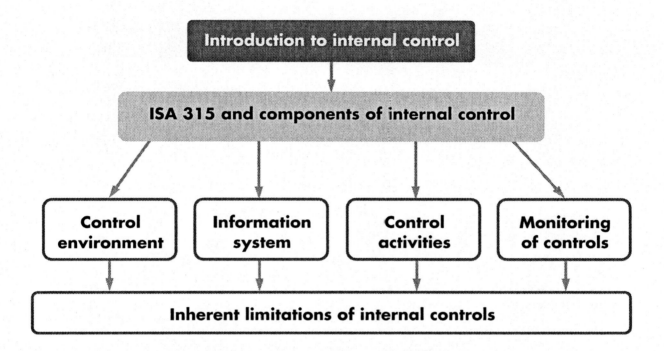

Introduction to internal control

ISA 315 and components of internal control

| Control environment | Information system | Control activities | Monitoring of controls |

Inherent limitations of internal controls

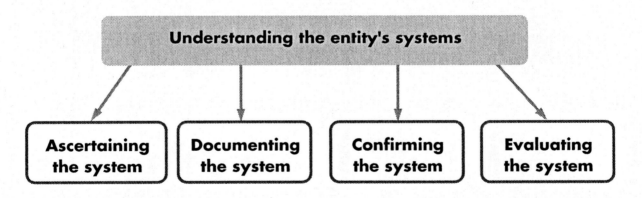

Main features of accounting systems

- Control objectives
- Risks
- Control procedures

Understanding the entity's systems

| Ascertaining the system | Documenting the system | Confirming the system | Evaluating the system |

1 Introduction to internal control

Internal control is the 'process designed, implemented and maintained by those charged with governance (the directors), management and other personnel to provide reasonable assurance about the achievement of an entity's objectives with regard to the reliability of financial reporting, effectiveness and efficiency of operations, and compliance with applicable laws and regulations. The term 'controls' refers to any aspects of one or more of the components of internal control' (ISA 315: para. 4 (c)).

As part of the audit, it is **imperative** to understand the controls in place within the client and the auditor does this at a relatively early stage in proceedings.

What is a control and how does it work?

Before we look at the precise definition, we need to understand what we mean by 'control' and how it might be 'in place' within the client.

Consider a **street light** – it is usually **in place** to meet the need of lighting a street at night for **safety and security purposes**. If we consider the darkened street it serves, there could be four situations in place:

> (1) The street light **does not exist** and the street is in darkness.
>
> (2) The street light **exists but is broken** (ie **not working properly**).
>
> (3) The street light **exists** but has a bulb that does not illuminate the street below (ie it is **ineffective**).
>
> (4) The street **light exists and illuminates the street effectively**, ensuring safety and security.

It is obvious that the auditor will need to understand the various controls in place within an entity to see which of these four states each control is in – here we will look at what **controls** there could be in a variety of systems and then consider the **processes** that auditors go through in order to assess them.

2 ISA 315 *Identifying and Assessing the Risks of Material Misstatement through Understanding of the Entity and its Environment*

'**Internal control** – The process designed, implemented and maintained by those charged with governance, management and other personnel to provide **reasonable assurance** about the achievement of an **entity's objectives** with regard to reliability of **financial reporting**, effectiveness and efficiency of **operations**, and **compliance** with applicable **laws and regulations**. The term "controls" refers to any aspects of one or more of the **components of internal control**.'

(ISA 315: para. 4c)

The ISA goes on to describe the components of internal control as the **control environment**, the entity's risk **assessment process**, the **information system**, **control activities** and **monitoring of controls** – these are all discussed below with the risk assessment process covered later on in your materials.

The other areas of the entity the auditor needs to understand are:

- Industry, regulatory, and other external factors, including the applicable financial reporting framework (such as suppliers, competitors, government and technology)

- Nature of the entity, including the entity's selection and application of accounting policies (plus the role that the various stakeholders play)

- Objectives and strategies and the related business risks that may result in a material misstatement of the financial statements

- Measurement and review of the entity's financial performance.

The last point (measurement and review of performance) is handled by an organisation's systems of internal control. In very broad terms, these internal control systems are designed to make sure that **good things** happen to an entity while **avoiding any bad things** at the same time. Not all entities have the same **approach** to setting up their internal controls, however, and this is frequently determined by the control environment – so what is the **control environment**?

2.1 Control environment

The **control environment** is 'the **attitudes, awareness,** and **actions** of those charged with governance and management concerning the entity's internal control and its importance in the entity' (ISA 315: para. A77).

> **ISA 315** uses the terms 'culture of honesty and ethical behaviour' as well as the 'importance' of internal controls within an organisation. This 'tone' is what influences 'the control consciousness of its people'. It stands to reason that the stronger the 'attitudes, awareness and actions of those charged with governance and management' in respect of the entity's internal controls, the better these internal controls will be (ISA 315: paras. 14 (a) and A77).

There are various ways that a **good control environment** can be seen in practice:

- Directors communicate and enforce integrity and ethical values.
- Directors and staff are committed to competence.
- Directors participate in control activities.
- Management operates in a way that promotes control.
- The organisation is structured in a way that promotes control.
- Authority and responsibility for controls is assigned to people.
- Human resources policies promote controls.

A **bad control environment** can be seen when the opposite of some of these is true; for example, directors who circumvent and ignore controls to get things done.

2.2 Information system

Within **information processing** controls, there are a number of specific controls that relate to **information technology** (IT) systems, although it must be remembered that an information system could just as easily be:

- A filing cabinet
- An integrated IT system.

According to ISA 315 (Appendix 1), the information system relevant to **financial reporting objectives**, which includes the financial reporting system, encompasses methods and records that:

- Identify and record all valid transactions

- Describe on a timely basis the transactions in sufficient detail to permit proper classification of transactions for financial reporting

- Measure the value of transactions in a manner that permits recording their proper monetary value in the financial statements

- Determine the time period in which transactions occurred to permit recording of transactions in the proper accounting period

- Present properly the transactions and related disclosures in the financial statements.

IT controls tend to be separated into two categories: **general** and **application**.

General IT controls	Application IT controls
Policies and **procedures** relating to many applications, **supporting** the **effective functioning** of application controls: • Data centre and **networks** • Systems software change, acquisition and maintenance • Program change • Access **security** • Application system acquisition, development and maintenance	Manual or automated procedures that apply to the **processing** of transactions. They can be both **preventative** and **detective** in nature: • Initiating, recording, processing and reporting **transactions** • Authorisation, completeness, and accuracy at all stages (eg input data, numerical sequence checks, **exception reports** and correction at point of data entry)

Activity 1: Computer controls

What additional controls would you expect to see in the client's computerised accounting system?

2.3 Control activities

Control activities are the policies and procedures that help ensure that management directives are carried out (they are often simply known as controls).

There are a variety of control activities that can be used by an organisation:

- Performance reviews – comparing budgets to actual performance

- Information processing – checking that transactions have been processed accurately, completely and have been authorised

- Physical controls – controls over the physical security of assets

- Segregation of duties – making sure that a number of people are involved in recording each transaction so that errors are noticed and there is less opportunity for individuals to carry out fraud

Control activities may include the following:

Authorisation of documents

Transactions should be authorised by an appropriate person, for example, overtime should be authorised by departmental heads.

Controls over computerised applications

These may be general controls or application controls (see above).

Controls over arithmetical accuracy

For example, when invoices are raised or received, a staff member should re-cast the amounts to ensure that the invoice adds up correctly.

Maintaining control accounts and trial balances

You should know from your accounting studies that these can be useful in ensuring errors have not been made in financial records, for example, some errors will result in a trial balance not balancing.

Reconciliations

Reconciling two different sources of information, such as a bank statement and a cashbook, or a purchase ledger account and a statement from the supplier can also highlight if errors have occurred.

Such a reconciliation may also involve comparing an external source of information with an internal source of information – another useful control on whether the internal source is correct.

Comparing assets to records

Again, this helps show if errors have been made in recording transactions or information. For example, staff might compare the physical non-current assets to what is recorded in the non-current asset register or the cash in the petty cash tin to what is in the petty cash book.

Restricting access (physical controls)

A good way of restricting errors and particularly fraud or theft is to restrict access to assets – for example, by locking receipts in a safe until they are deposited at the bank, having codes to unlock the cash tills, locking the stores where inventory is kept.

A **strong control environment** is demonstrated by having sound **control activities**.

Activity 2: Control activities

Required

Select examples for each of the specified control activities from the picklist.

Performance reviews		▼
Information processing		▼
Physical controls		▼
Segregation of duties		▼

Picklist:

Security staff at a warehouse

Budgetary control meetings

Separate staff for counting, banking and recording cash

Agreeing the sales ledger total to a batch of authorised invoices

2.4 Monitoring of controls

A further component of a good system of internal control is **monitoring** – those activities that the entity uses to **keep an eye on** how well it is **achieving its objectives** and how the entity initiates **remedial action** to **address deficiencies** in control. Examples of monitoring include:

- **Management** controls such as reviewing whether a bank reconciliation is prepared on a timely basis and following up on any areas of non-compliance. Such controls can be either **preventative controls** (designed to reduce the occurrence of errors and deviations – eg secure storage of inventory in a warehouse) or **detective controls** (designed to identify errors and deviations once they have occurred – eg a burglar alarm). Monitoring the effectiveness of each will help an entity decide whether it requires more of one or the other when establishing controls.

- **Internal audit** (a specific department within an entity that monitors all aspects of the entity and reports its findings to those charged with governance)

- Other governance arrangements (such as the use of an audit committee staffed with **non-executive directors** representing the interests of shareholders)

- **Information systems** designed not only to report but also to interrogate data

- **Communication channels** with **stakeholders** (eg customer feedback or liaison with regulators)

2.5 Inherent limitations of internal controls

However, good any single element of an internal control system might be, an internal control system can never be perfect, due to inherent limitations.

Internal controls are usually designed to operate **as effectively as the entity considers appropriate** in the context of its **control environment**. However, just as the auditor can only offer reasonable assurance on the work they have done during the audit, the internal controls in place within an entity can only provide **reasonable assurance** that they will achieve the entity's **objectives**. In other words, there are always going to be **some inherent limitations of internal controls** (ISA 315: paras. A54–56).

Activity 3: Internal control inherent limitations

Required

In what ways might a system of internal controls contain inherent limitations?

As we saw in the previous activity, there is a risk that the **integrity** of **management** might have an impact on the **control environment**. The auditor needs to take this into account when **planning** the audit and **designing procedures** to assess the truth and fairness of the financial statements. The use of **feedback** from management, including **system weaknesses**, clerical or accounting **mistakes** and **disagreements** over accounting policies or treatment, can assist the auditor when planning the audit by **highlighting issues** to be on the lookout for.

3 The main features of accounting systems

3.1 Introduction

You know from your AAT studies already that an entity manages its own financial stability by having a collection of **systems** in place. Specific examples of such systems will follow but, for all of them, in order to reach a valid conclusion for the opinion, for each system the auditor needs to be able to understand control objectives, risks and control procedures:

(1) **Control objectives** (what a system is trying to do)
(2) **Risks** (what a system is trying to avoid)
(3) **Control procedures** (how a system achieves objectives and manages risks)

Activity 4: Control objectives, risks and procedures – introduction

Required

For each of the following, select whether it is a control objective, a control activity, or a test of control, using the options listed below.

Observe post opening		▼
Safeguard blank purchase order forms		▼
Review numerical sequence of goods received notes		▼

Picklist:

Control activity
Control objective
Test of control

The following is a list of the major accounting systems that you will need to know about:

> - Purchases
> - Revenue
> - Payroll
> - Inventory
> - Non-current assets
> - Cash and bank

Activity 5: Control objectives, risks and procedures for systems

Required

For each of the main accounting systems, can you think of some examples of control objectives, risks and control procedures?

	Control objectives	Risks	Control procedures
Purchases			
Revenue			
Payroll			
Inventory			
Non-current assets			
Cash and bank			

4 Understanding the entity's systems

Previously we saw how **controls** played a big part in making sure that accounting and other information systems helped entities **achieve their objectives**. The auditor needs to **understand these systems** and **controls** in order to reach a **conclusion** about the truth and fairness of the financial statements that they help to create. **ISA 315** states:

'The auditor shall obtain an understanding of the information system, including the related business processes, relevant to financial reporting, including the following areas:

(a) The **classes of transactions** in the entity's operations that are significant to the financial statements

> Understanding the various transactions of an entity (eg inflows and outflows) makes it easier for the auditor to reach a conclusion about it. Procedures can be both manual and automated – we will look at how to audit IT systems later in the course.

(b) The **procedures**, within both **information technology** (IT) and **manual systems**, by which those transactions are initiated, recorded, processed, corrected as necessary, transferred to the general ledger and reported in the financial statements

> Procedures can be both manual or automated – we will look at how to audit IT systems later in the Course Book.

(c) The **related accounting records**, supporting information and specific accounts in the financial statements that are used to initiate, record, process and report transactions; this includes the **correction of incorrect information** and how information is transferred to the general ledger. The records may be in either manual or electronic form

> Auditors need to understand the various documents used – invoices, reports, payment authorisations etc.

(d) How the information system **captures events** and **conditions**, other than transactions, that are significant to the financial statements

> Part of the auditor's job is to observe how systems capture such data to ensure they are recorded effectively.

(e) The **financial reporting process** used to prepare the entity's financial statements, including **significant accounting estimates** and **disclosures**

> How many estimates are used in producing a set of financial statements?

(f) Controls surrounding **journal entries**, including non-standard journal entries used to record **non-recurring**, **unusual transactions** or **adjustments**.'

> Auditors must make sure that there is sound judgement behind all entries on the main ledgers, including journals.

(ISA 315: para. 18)

We are now going to look at how the auditor gains an understanding of such systems from the following procedures:

- Ascertaining the accounting system
- Documenting the accounting system
- Confirming the accounting system
- Evaluating the accounting system

4.1 Ascertaining the accounting system

Activity 6: Ascertaining the accounting system

Required

What methods can the auditor use to understand the accounting system?

4.2 Documenting the accounting system

There are **three methods** commonly used to document the client's accounting system:

- **Narrative notes**: written descriptions of the system.

- **Internal control checklists (ICCs)** or **internal control questionnaires (ICQs)**: the audit firm will have a standard list of control questions for each type of system in place. The audit staff can quickly ascertain which, if any, are in operation by the client.

- **Flowcharts**: diagrammatic representations of the system, usually broken down into separate activities.

Narrative notes

These are a good way of getting an overview of a particular activity. They are not always appropriate, as this illustration attempts to demonstrate:

Illustration 1

Three pieces of information need to be recorded – which of the three techniques described above would work best to document the system of recording each piece of information?

Your child's performance at school	Directions to your house	Instructions for completion of a passport application

Narrative notes work well for all of these tasks, but you may find that something **visual** like a **flowchart** works better for directions and instructions. In the case of **directions**, a **map** often works well and, to ensure that all parts of the **passport application** are completed appropriately, a **checklist** of items that should have been done would work well. **Simple tasks** are often recorded best using narrative notes, which is what the auditor will do first.

Internal control checklists or questionnaires

Activity 7: Internal control questionnaire

Required

Use the accounting system information for sales at Glad Rags Limited given below to complete the internal control questionnaire laid out in the solution space.

Accounting system information – Revenue system

The company manufactures clothes to order from a catalogue. When an order is received, the sales department checks that the customer has not exceeded their credit limit and then issues a two-part order document. The sales department fill in the appropriate values for the order from current price lists. One copy is sent to the production department in order for the order to be completed and the other is filed alphabetically in the customer file in the sales department.

Once the order is completed, two-part despatch notes are raised. When the factory manager, Ian Jones, has checked the order, one copy of the despatch note is despatched with the goods (to be signed and returned), and one part is matched to the production department's sales order and sent to accounts to raise the invoice. Jane Hill raises the invoices from the order and despatch note, enters them on the computer and sends them out to customers.

Most customers pay in around 60 days. When they come in, cheques are passed to Beth Simpkins, one of the accounts assistants, and she updates the cash book and the sales ledger. Cheques are banked twice a week. Cheques are kept securely in the safe until banking.

Jane sends out statements to customers each month. Glad Rags' customers are mostly all reputable high street stores and there are rarely irrecoverable debts.

Internal control questionnaire – Revenue and Receivables system

Question	Yes/No	Comment
Are orders only accepted from low credit risks?		
Are despatches checked by appropriate personnel?		
Are goods sent out recorded?		
Are customers required to give evidence of receipt of goods?		
Are invoices checked to despatch notes and orders?		
Are invoices prepared using authorised prices?		
Are invoices checked to ensure they add up correctly?		
Are sales receipts matched with invoices?		
Are statements sent out regularly?		
Are overdue accounts reviewed regularly?		
Are there safeguards over post received to ensure that cheques are not intercepted?		
Are bankings made daily?		
Would it be appropriate to perform tests of control here?		

Flowcharts

Flowcharts should be kept **simple** and be **clear to read**. The following points should help:

- There should be conformity of symbols, with each symbol representing one thing.

- There should be a key of symbols used.

- The chart should flow from top to bottom and from left to right, with no loose ends.

- Connecting lines should only cross where necessary in order to keep the chart simple.

Illustration 2: A list of basic flowcharting symbols

eg Sales Invoice (SI)	Document (eg Sales invoice)
N / eg Delivery Note DN	Document sequentially numbered
eg GRN	3 part document
eg SL	Account book or ledger
A D N (triangle)	File A = alphabetical order D = date order N = numerical order T = temporary (TN would be temporary in numerical order.)
✕	An operation (but not a check)
◇	A check function
③	A connector (ie to page 3 of the flowchart)
───────▶	Document flow (ie between departments)
- - - - - - -▶	Information flow (ie information is often transferred from one document to another)

An **example** of a flowchart is shown below:

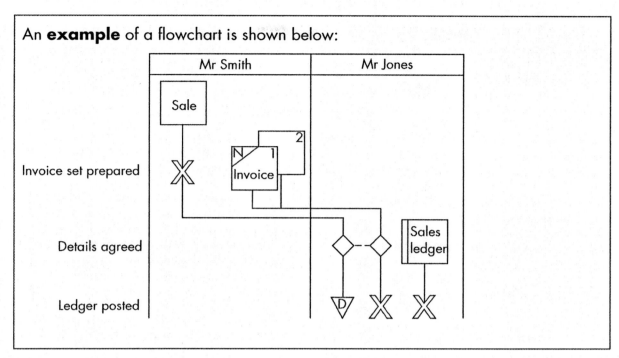

Activity 8: Documenting systems

Required

From the picklist, select one advantage and one disadvantage for each of the three techniques used to document the client's accounting system.

	Advantages	Disadvantages
Narrative notes	▼	▼
Flowcharts	▼	▼
Questionnaires	▼	▼

Picklists:

Client may overstate controls
Confusing if system is complex
Easier to interpret for larger, more complex systems
Easy to delegate to junior staff
Need experience to prepare
Quick to prepare

4.3 Confirming the accounting system

The auditor will confirm the system by performing **walk-through tests**. This involves following one or more transactions of each type through the accounting system to **confirm** that the system has been documented properly.

4.4 Evaluating the accounting system

The auditor must then **evaluate** the system to identify the factors that contribute to strengths and deficiencies in accounting systems. This evaluation must consider the **presence** or **absence** of internal controls, including their impacts, plus an evaluation of the **design** and also the **operation** of the system. The evaluation is undertaken by conducting a series of **tests** of the system, recording the results for feeding into the overall audit strategy and, where appropriate, reporting any weaknesses in controls back to the client.

We saw earlier that systems and controls could be both manual and IT based, so we will look at how auditors review both types of system later on in this chapter.

Following on from **confirmation** of the system (obtained via **walk-through tests**, above) the auditor will generally come to one of two conclusions about the client's systems:

- If they believe controls are effective, they will test them using **tests of control** and take a combined approach to the audit, where they test both controls and **balances** in the financial statements (we will see more of this balance-led or **'substantive' approach** later).

- If they do not believe the controls are effective, they will not bother testing them and carry out **substantive testing** only instead, which involves testing **balances** and **transactions** in more detail.

Activity 9: Evaluating systems

Required

Read the following narrative notes for the revenue system at MEM Ltd and then consider the two tasks below.

'Sales orders are taken by the sales department, usually by phone. The sales department consists of the sales director, Ted Bishop, and his assistant, Sandra Dales. When they take an order from an existing customer, they check that the customer does not have outstanding orders which exceed the credit limit on the account. They then record the order on a three-part, pre-numbered sales order document. Only Ted is allowed to authorise individual sales orders in excess of £20,000.

When a new customer makes an order, Sandra passes the query to Ted, who carries out a credit check before the order is accepted and then sets a credit limit based on that check. Only then is the order accepted and processed.

One copy of the sales order is filed in the client file in the sales department, and two are sent to the production department to start work on the order. The production controller, Ben Swales, determines when the order can be fulfilled by, which is written on the two copies of the sales order. One is then sent to the customer and the other is retained in the 'orders pending' file in Ben's office until the order has been completed.

When the order is ready to be despatched, Ben checks the date and, if the order has been completed early, telephones the customer to ensure it is okay to despatch the order. Before goods are despatched, they are checked for quality and quantity against the order by Ian Mellor, the factory foreman. He then completes a two-part, pre-numbered goods despatch note. One copy is sent out to the customer with the goods; the other, stamped 'despatched', is matched with the production copy of the sales order and sent to the accounts department. Goods are not despatched after 3pm.

At 3:30pm, in the accounts department, Tessa Goodyear raises the invoices based on the goods despatch notes she has been sent by the production department. The invoices are created on the computer by her entering the appropriate details. The computer gives her a sequential number for each invoice. Prices are automatically inserted on the invoice from the price list when she inputs the inventory number. If a special price has been negotiated, this will be stated on the sales order attached to the goods despatch note, and she will have to manually override the price given by the computer. She prints off the invoices and checks that they are calculated correctly. One copy of the invoice is matched with the order and GDN and filed, numerically, in the accounts department. The other copy is sent out. The computer automatically updates a sales day book and the sales ledger for the invoiced sales. Sometimes not all the invoices are completed until the next morning. The invoices are always sent out in one batch.

The accounts department receives the post at 10am, when it has been sorted by the managing director's secretary. The post is opened by Tessa Goodyear and Paula Taylor, the cashier, who makes a list of all the sales ledger receipts. The cheques are placed in the safe until they are banked in the afternoon, by Paula Taylor. Paula then enters the receipts in the cash book on the computer. The cash book program automatically updates the sales ledger.

The financial controller, Marie Edgehill, reconciles the sales ledger control account on a monthly basis.

Every Monday, Tessa Goodyear prints an aged receivables report off the sales ledger and reviews it for potentially irrecoverable debts. She then takes appropriate action, which is usually to highlight potential problems to Marie, or to telephone customers to ask when they are going to be able to pay. In rare circumstances, MEM uses a debt collection service to enforce very late debts.'

Task 1

Identify five control procedures operating in this system.

(1)

(2)

(3)

(4)

(5)

Task 2

Using the options listed below, state whether the following are strengths or deficiencies of MEM's system or potentially both.

Only Ted Bishop is allowed to authorise new customers and orders over £20,000.	▼
Orders are recorded on pre-numbered sales orders.	▼
Goods are sometimes ready for despatch early.	▼
It is necessary for Tessa to manually override the price system on the computer if a special price has been negotiated.	▼

Picklist:

Deficiency
Potentially both
Strength

Recording and communicating the results of testing

Once the auditor has completed work on testing controls, the **results** are recorded as **evidence** and retained for the purposes we described earlier using ISA 230 *Audit Documentation*. They will also be used by the auditor to **revisit** the overall **audit strategy** and the **audit plan** to establish if any **changes** are required in the light of such evidence. It is entirely likely that the audit will 'evolve' during the course of this process, reinforcing the need for auditors to stay **alert** to all the evidence they uncover.

Chapter summary

- Internal control is the process designed, implemented and maintained by those charged with governance (the directors), management and other personnel, to provide reasonable assurance about the achievement of the entity's objectives with regard to the reliability of financial reporting, effectiveness and efficiency of operations; and compliance with applicable laws and regulations.

- Auditors use ISA 315 to gain an understanding of the various components of internal control relevant to forming an opinion on the financial statements of their clients. These are:

  - The control environment
  - The entity's risk assessment process
  - The information system (both general and application controls)
  - Control activities
  - Monitoring of controls

- No matter how well designed a system of internal controls might be, there will always be inherent limitations of that system (including human error, fraud and even freak occurrences).

- The main features of any accounting system (including purchases, revenue, payroll, inventory, non-current assets and cash and bank) are designed to take account of the 'system's control objectives, the risks they are trying to avoid and the control procedures designed to assure the former and manage the latter.

- When understanding an entity's systems, an auditor will focus on four main areas:

  - Ascertaining the system

  - Documenting the system (using a variety of activities such as questionnaires, checklists and flowcharts)

  - Confirming the system via walk-through testing

  - Evaluating the system (either strengths or weaknesses)

- Recording and communicating the results of these activities inform the rest of the audit and are documented thoroughly to ensure the audit is effective.

- **Control activities:** the policies and procedures that help ensure that management directives are carried out (they are often simply known as controls)

- **Control environment:** the attitudes, awareness and actions of management and those charged with governance regarding internal control and its importance

- **Control objectives:** what a system is trying to do

- **Control procedures:** how a system achieves objectives and manages risks

- **Internal control:** the process used by a client to prevent, detect and report risks and achieve objectives regarding operations, compliance with laws and regulations and safeguarding assets

- **Inherent limitations of internal controls:** however good any single element of an internal control system might be, an internal control system can never be perfect, due to inherent limitations

- **Risks:** what a system is trying to avoid

Test your learning

1   Complete the statement below describing an internal control system.

Internal control is the process [▼], implemented and [▼] by [▼], [▼] and other personnel to provide [▼] about the achievement of the entity's [▼] with regard to the reliability of [▼], effectiveness and efficiency of [▼] and compliance with applicable laws and regulations.

Picklist for line items:

Designed
Financial reporting
Maintained
Management
Objectives
Operations
Reasonable assurance
Those charged with governance

2   Accounting systems have control objectives and control procedures to mitigate the risk that the control objective is not met.

For each of the following, select whether they are a control objective, risk, or control procedure.

A company should only pay for work done by employees.	▼
Company vehicles are used by employees for their own purposes.	▼
Part C39t99, in regular use in the business, is reordered when inventory levels fall below 200.	▼

Picklist:

Control objective
Control procedure
Risk

3   State whether the following statements are true or false in respect of a company's control environment.

The directors can ensure a good control environment by implementing controls themselves and never bypassing them.		▼
The directors should not assign authority for control areas to members of staff.		▼
A good control environment always leads to a good system of control overall.		▼

Picklist:

True
False

4   Select which one of the following statements concerning small and large companies is the least true by ticking the appropriate box.

Control activities will be similar in all sizes of company over core activities. ☐

A large company is likely to have a more formal control system than a small company. ☐

A small company is likely to have a less complex information system than a big company. ☐

A large company is more likely to have a good control environment than a small company. ☐

5   Select which one of the following best describes who undertakes the role of monitoring controls at a company by ticking the appropriate box.

Controls are always monitored by an internal audit function, as this is the purpose of their existence. ☐

Controls are monitored by the directors of a company. ☐

Controls are monitored by the people who operate them, as they are in the best position to assess whether the objectives of the controls are being met. ☐

Who monitors controls depends on the size of the company and its personnel: it may be an internal audit function, but it could also be the directors, or department heads. ☐

6 The personnel director at Metal Extrusions Midlands Limited (MEM) has contacted the audit firm and said that she wants to overhaul the internal control system over wages and salaries at MEM. All members of staff (waged and salaried) are paid by bank transfer. Waged staff members are paid weekly and salaried staff members are paid monthly. At present, the payroll is prepared and authorised by the personnel director, who has sole access to employee records. The bank transfer is authorised by the personnel director but enacted by the cashier.

Set out the control objectives that the personnel director of MEM should consider when putting together a new control system for wages and salaries.

7 Listed below are two control procedures that the directors have put into action at MEM as a result of your recommendations.

For each internal control procedure, use the picklist below to match the procedure with the control objective.

Internal control procedure	
The payroll should be reconciled to other records, such as the cash payment for net pay per the bank's records.	▼
The payroll should be authorised by someone other than the personnel director.	▼

Picklist:

Employees should only be paid for work done.
Gross pay, net pay and deductions should be correctly recorded on payroll.
Gross pay should be calculated correctly and authorised.
Wages and salaries should be recorded properly in bank records.

8 An entity uses internal control procedures in order to mitigate the risk to which it is exposed. Listed below are two internal control procedures which are applicable to an entity's non-current assets system.

For each internal control procedure, use the picklist below to match the procedure with the risk mitigated.

Internal control procedure	
Non-current assets are inspected regularly.	▼
Capital expenditure is approved by the purchasing director on behalf of the board.	▼

Picklist:

Assets are bought from inappropriate suppliers at inflated cost.
Assets are depreciated incorrectly.
Assets are not maintained properly for use in the business.
Assets are sold when they are needed for use in the business.

9 An entity uses internal control procedures in order to mitigate the risk to which it is exposed. Listed below are two internal control procedures which are applicable to an entity's inventory system.

For each internal control procedure, use the picklist below to match the procedure with the risk mitigated.

Internal control procedure	
Inventory store is kept locked.	▼
Goods inwards are checked for quality.	▼

Picklist:

Damaged inventory is valued in the financial statements.
Inventory is counted in the financial statements without a corresponding payable.
Inventory is stolen.
The company fails to order required goods.

10 External auditors use a variety of methods for documenting systems of control, including flowcharts, internal control questionnaires and checklists.

For each of the following descriptions, select whether it represents a flowchart, internal control questionnaire or internal control checklist.

A series of questions designed to identify controls in a system. A 'no' answer indicates a deficiency in controls	▼
A graphic rendition of the system, using conventional symbols to represent controls and documents	▼

Picklist:

Flowchart
Internal Control Checklist
Internal Control Questionnaire

Appendix

Accounting systems – control objectives, risks and control procedures

Purchases

Control objective	Risk	Control procedures
Ordering		
A company should only order goods and services that are authorised by appropriate personnel and are for the company's benefit	The company pays for unnecessary or personal goods	Orders should be authorised only when the need for the items has been justified (on a purchase requisition, for example)
		Orders should only be prepared when authorised purchase requisitions are received from departments
		Orders should be authorised by separate officers (segregation of duties)
		Orders should be pre-numbered and blank order forms should be safeguarded
		Orders not yet received should be reviewed
A company should only order from authorised suppliers	Other suppliers may not supply quality goods or may be too expensive	A company should have a central policy for choosing suppliers

Control objective	Risk	Control procedures
Receipt of goods and invoices		
A company should ensure that goods and services received are used for the organisation's purposes	The company may pay for goods/services for personal use	Goods received should be examined for quality and quantity
A company should only accept goods that have been ordered (and appropriately authorised)	The company may pay for goods/services for personal use	Goods received should be recorded on pre-numbered goods received notes
A company should record all goods and services received	The company fails to pay for goods/services and loses suppliers	Goods received notes should be compared with purchase orders by different staff (segregation of duties)
A company should not acknowledge liability for goods it has not recorded	The company pays for goods it has not received	Supplier invoices should be checked to orders and goods received notes
		Supplier invoices should be referenced (numerical order and supplier reference)
		Supplier invoices should be checked for prices, quantities, calculations
A company should ensure it claims all credits due to it	The company pays for poor-quality goods	There should be procedures for obtaining credit notes from suppliers
		Goods returned should be recorded on pre-numbered goods returned notes

Control objective	Risk	Control procedures
Accounting		
A company should only make authorised payments for goods that have been received	The company pays for goods it has not received	Payments should be authorised and only made if goods have been received The purchase ledger control account should be reconciled to the list of balances on a regular basis
A company should record expenditure accurately in the accounting records	The financial statements are misstated, and the company does not pay for genuine liabilities	Purchases and purchases returns should be promptly recorded in day books and ledgers.
A company should record credit notes received correctly in the accounting records	The financial statements are misstated, and the company pays for items unnecessarily	The purchase ledger should be regularly maintained
A company should record liabilities in the correct purchase ledger accounts	The company pays the wrong supplier	Supplier statements should be compared with the purchase ledger
A company should record liabilities in the correct period	The financial statements are misstated by recording purchases but not inventory, or recording inventory but not the associated purchase liability	Goods received but not yet invoiced at the year end should be accrued separately

Control objective	Risk	Control procedures
Payment		
A company should only make payments to the correct recipients and for the correct amounts which are authorised	The company pays the wrong supplier	Cheques should be requisitioned and requests evidenced with supporting documentation
A company should only pay for liabilities once	The company pays more than once and the supplier does not correct the error	Cheque payments should be authorised by someone other than a signatory
		There should be limitations on the payment amount individual staff members can sign for
		Blank cheques should never be signed
		Signed cheques should be despatched promptly
		Paid cheques should be collected from the bank (ie after the supplier has banked them, the company can get them back as proof)
		Electronic payments should be set up for payment and then separately authorised by another officer of the company (segregation of duties)
		Electronic payment limits should be established through the banking software to ensure that large payments require at least two banking authorisations
		The bank statement should be regularly reconciled to the cash book
		Cash payments should be limited and authorised
		Payments should be recorded promptly in the cash book and ledger

Revenue

Control objective	Risk	Control procedures
Orders and extending credit		
A company should only supply goods to customers who are likely to pay for them	Selling to customers who do not have a good credit rating	Credit terms offered to customers should be authorised by senior personnel and reviewed regularly
A company should encourage customers to pay promptly	The company loses the value of being able to use the money in their business or interest on the money in the bank due to late payment	Credit checks should be run on new customers
		Changes in customer data (for example, their address) should be authorised by senior personnel
A company should record orders correctly	The company sends the wrong goods to the customer, causing added cost or risk of loss of the customer	Orders should only be accepted from customers with no existing payment problems after confirming that those customers are within their existing credit limit
A company should fulfil orders promptly/in full	The company loses custom	Order documents should be sequentially numbered so that false or missing sales can be traced
Despatching and invoicing goods		
A company should record all goods it sends out	Goods are sent out and not invoiced, and the company loses money	Despatch of goods should be authorised by appropriate personnel and checked back to order documents (segregation of duties)
A company should invoice all goods and services sold correctly	Insufficient sums are charged and the company loses money	Despatched goods should be checked for quality and quantity
A company should only invoice goods it has sent out	The company charges for goods in error and loses custom	Goods sent out should be

Control objective	Risk	Control procedures
A company should only issue credit notes where required	The company issues credit notes incorrectly and loses money	recorded
		Records of sent out goods should be agreed to customer orders, despatch notes and invoices by separate staff (segregation of duties)
		Despatch notes should be sequentially numbered and the sequence checked regularly
		Returned goods should be checked for quality
		Returned goods should be recorded on goods returned notes
		Customers should sign despatch notes as proof of receipt
		Invoices should be prepared using authorised prices and quantities and should be checked to despatch notes
		Invoices should be checked to ensure they add up correctly
		Credit notes should be authorised by appropriate personnel
		Invoices and credit notes should be pre-numbered and the sequence checked regularly
		Inventory records should be updated from goods sent out records
		Sales invoices should be matched with signed delivery notes and sales orders
		Orders not yet delivered should be regularly reviewed

Control objective	Risk	Control procedures
Recording and accounting for revenue, credit control		
A company should record all invoiced revenue in its accounting records ie sales ledger and general ledger	Revenue is not recorded and wrongly omitted from financial statements, and payment is not chased as sale was never recorded	Sales invoice sequence should be recorded and spoilt invoices recorded and destroyed
A company should record all credit notes in its accounting records	As above, financial statements likely to be misstated and potential to lose custom by chasing cancelled debts	Sales receipts should be matched with invoices by separate staff (segregation of duties) Customer remittance advices should be retained
A company should record all invoiced revenue in the correct sales ledger accounts	Losing custom by chasing the wrong customer for the debt and not receiving the money from the correct customer	Sales returns and price adjustments should be recorded separately from the original sale
A company must ensure that invoices are recorded in the sales ledger in the correct time period	Errors in the financial statements due to counting both the sale and the related inventory as assets or counting neither	Procedures should exist to record revenue in the correct period Receivable statements should be prepared regularly Receivable statements should be checked regularly
A company must identify debts for which payment might be doubtful	The company fails to take action until it is too late to retrieve the debt and, in the worst case, wrongly records irrecoverable debts as assets in the financial statements	Receivable statements should be safeguarded so they cannot be amended before they are sent out Overdue accounts should be reviewed and followed up Write-off of irrecoverable debts should be authorised by appropriate personnel The sales ledger control account should be reconciled regularly The sales ledger and profit margins should be analysed regularly

Control objective	Risk	Control procedures
Receiving payment (cash)		
A company should record all money received	Money could be stolen or lost, custom could be lost through chasing payments already made by the customer, the financial statements are likely to be misstated	There should be safeguards to protect post received to avoid interception (segregation of duties)
A company should bank all money received	Money could be stolen or lost with consequences, as above, or the company loses out on interest that could be being made on receipts	Two people should be present at post opening, a list of receipts should be made and post should be stamped with the date opened (segregation of duties) There should be restrictions on who is allowed to accept cash (cashiers or salespeople)
A company should safeguard money received in the period until it is banked	Money may be stolen in the interim period	Cash received should be evidenced (till rolls, receipts) Cash registers should be regularly emptied Till rolls should be reconciled to cash collections which should then be agreed to bankings by separate staff (segregation of duties) Cash shortages should be investigated Cash records should be maintained promptly There should be appropriate arrangements made when cashiers are on holiday Receipts books should be serially numbered and kept locked up Bankings should be made daily Paying-in books should be compared to initial cash records

Control objective	Risk	Control procedures
		All receipts should be banked together
		Opening of new bank accounts should be restricted and authorised
		Cash floats held should be limited
		There should be restrictions on making payments from cash received and restricted access to cash held on the premises
		Cash floats should be checked by an independent person sometimes on a surprise basis
		Cash should be locked up outside hours

Payroll

Control objective	Risk	Control procedures
Setting pay		
A company should only pay employees for work they have done	The company overpays employees	Personnel records should be kept; and wages and salaries checked to details held in them
A company should pay employees the correct gross pay, which has previously been authorised		Personnel files should be kept locked up
		Engaging employees, setting rates of pay, changing rates of pay, overtime, non-statutory deductions from pay and advances of pay should all be authorised and recorded by separate staff members (segregation of duties)
		Changes in personnel and pay rates should be recorded
		Hours worked should be recorded; time should be clocked
		Hours worked should be reviewed
		Payroll should be reviewed against budget
Recording wages and salaries		
A company should record gross pay, net pay, and relevant deductions correctly on the payroll	The company may make incorrect payments to staff/tax offices and financial statements may be misstated	Payroll should be prepared, checked and approved before payment
A company should record payments made in the cash and bank records and general ledger	The financial statements may be misstated	
A company should comply with the requirements of the Data Protection Act 1998	The company could make unauthorised disclosures of employee information	

Control objective	Risk	Control procedures
Paying wages and salaries		
A company should pay the correct employees	Angry, unpaid workforce and/or the company overpays the wrong people	Wage cheques for cash payments should be authorised
		Cash should be kept securely
		Identity of staff should be verified before payment
		Distributions of cash wages should be recorded and undertaken by two employees (segregation of duties)
		Bank transfer lists should be prepared and authorised
		Bank transfer lists should be compared to the payroll
Deductions		
A company should ensure all deductions have been properly calculated and authorised	Breaking the law, calculating staff pensions incorrectly leading to staff displeasure	Separate employee records should be maintained
		Total pay and deductions should be reconciled month on month
A company should ensure it pays the correct amounts to taxation authorities	Breaking the law and incurring fines	Costs of pay should be compared to budgets
		Gross pay and total tax deducted should be checked to returns to the tax authorities

Inventory

Control objective	Risk	Control procedures
Recording of inventory		
Inventory movements authorised and recorded	Inventory might be stolen	Segregation of duties between custody of inventory and recording
Inventory records only include items that belong to the company or that exist at all	Inventory may be overstated in the financial statements	Checking and recording goods inwards
Inventory quantities have been recorded correctly	The company may have insufficient inventory to operate efficiently and inventory may be misstated in the financial statements	Issues of inventory supported by appropriate documentation
Inventory is not recorded as an asset once a sale has been made or before a purchase is recognised	The financial statements may be misstated	Maintaining inventory records
Protection of inventory		
Inventory is protected from loss/damage	Goods might be stolen or unusable/unsaleable	Restriction of access to stores Controls on stores environment (temperature/damp etc) Regular inventory counts by independent people Reconciliation of inventory count to book records
Valuation of inventory		
Inventory is valued correctly	Inventory may be misstated in the financial statements	Calculation of inventory value and checking of calculation
Slow-moving, obsolete and damaged inventory is noted	Inventory may be overstated in the financial statements	Regular review of inventory condition Accounting for scrap and waste

Control objective	Risk	Control procedures
Inventory levels		
Levels of inventory held are reasonable	The company may not have sufficient inventory to function efficiently	Maximum and minimum inventory levels set Reorder limits set

Non-current assets

Control objective	Risk	Control procedures
Buying assets		
Non-current asset additions are authorised	The company buys assets it does not need and/or at an inappropriate price	Capital expenditure is budgeted for/authorised by a senior official in the company (segregation of duties)
Storing and using assets		
Non-current assets are kept securely	The assets are stolen	A non-current asset register is maintained and compared with actual assets and general ledger record of assets Non-current assets are inspected regularly to ensure they are maintained/in use/secure
Non-current assets are maintained properly	The assets are not fit for use in the business when required	
Selling assets		
Non-current asset disposals are authorised	The company sells assets it needs to operate and/or at an inappropriate price	Non-current asset sales or scrappage is authorised/planned to avoid business interruption

Control objective	Risk	Control procedures
Recording assets		
Non-current assets are properly accounted for and recorded	The company misstates non-current assets in the financial statements	Rates at which depreciation is charged are authorised/ checked
Rate at which depreciation is charged is reasonable	Assets are valued wrongly and financial statements are misstated	Non-current asset register is maintained
Proceeds from disposal of non-current assets are recorded	Proceeds may be stolen or omitted from financial statements, profit or loss on sale of assets may be misstated in financial statements	

Cash and bank

Control objective	Risk	Control procedures
All cash should be held securely both in hand and at the bank	Cash is misappropriated through either fraud or error	Controls to ensure the completeness of recording cash receipts
All receipts and payments should be recorded	Lack of visibility over transactions and balances	Post-opening procedures to ensure all remittances are complete (including segregation of duties)
Staff should be accountable for all cash transactions and balances	Transactions and changes to cash held and in bank accounts occur without authorisation	Restrictions over who can receive cash, how they evidence cash receipts and regular reconciliations of receipts
The organisation should have the cash available that it needs	Being unable to pay bills as they fall due and incurring costs for having insufficient funds available	Paying cash and cheques into the bank promptly
		Reconciliation of funds received via electronic funds transfer at point of sale (EFTPOS) to ensure completeness
		Physical controls over blank cheques and limited access to creating system-generated payments (such as BACS)

Control objective	Risk	Control procedures
		Petty cash controls (physical, authorisation, recording)
		Cash flow forecasts and monitoring procedures to ensure cash needs are met

Obtaining audit evidence

3

Learning outcomes

4.1	**Evaluate methods used to obtain audit evidence in a given situation**
	• Types of verification techniques (inspection, observation, external confirmation, recalculation, re-performance, analytical procedures and enquiry)
	• When it is appropriate to use each type of verification technique
	• Reliability of different sources of audit evidence
	• Differences between tests of controls and substantive procedures
	• Methods used to test controls, transactions and balances
	• Assertions
4.2	**Evaluate audit techniques used in an IT environment**
	• Use computer-assisted audit techniques (CAATs), including test data, integrated test facilities and audit software, to test controls and interrogate the audited entity's files
	• Identify the benefits and drawbacks of using CAATs.
4.3	**Evaluate and use different sampling techniques**
	• Distinguish between statistical and non-statistical sampling
	• Determine when it is more appropriate to examine 100% or a selection of items
	• Distinguish between selection methods and when they should be used
	• Identify factors affecting sample sizes
	• Identify appropriate populations from which to select samples.
4.4	**Develop an audit approach suitable for a given situation**
	• Establish why auditors need to understand the audited entity's internal controls
	• Determine when to use a mixture of tests of controls and substantive procedures or substantive procedures only
	• Identify why it is appropriate to use a mixture of tests of controls and substantive procedures or substantive procedures only.
4.5	**Select procedures for a given assertion**
	• Apply audit procedures to test financial statement assertions.

Assessment context

Five separate tasks from the assessment will be addressed by this topic as we look at how to obtain audit evidence. Remember that objective test questions can take many forms, not just multiple choice.

Qualification context

There are some new pieces of terminology introduced here – evidence, sampling and computer audit – but although they are all new, they exist in areas that you have seen elsewhere in your AAT studies (such as final accounts and accounting software).

Business context

Evidence is the oxygen without which the auditor cannot breathe: the more of it there is, the more likely it is that the auditor is able to achieve their overall objective – providing an audit opinion. In the real world, the collection of evidence is the most time-consuming part of any audit.

Chapter overview

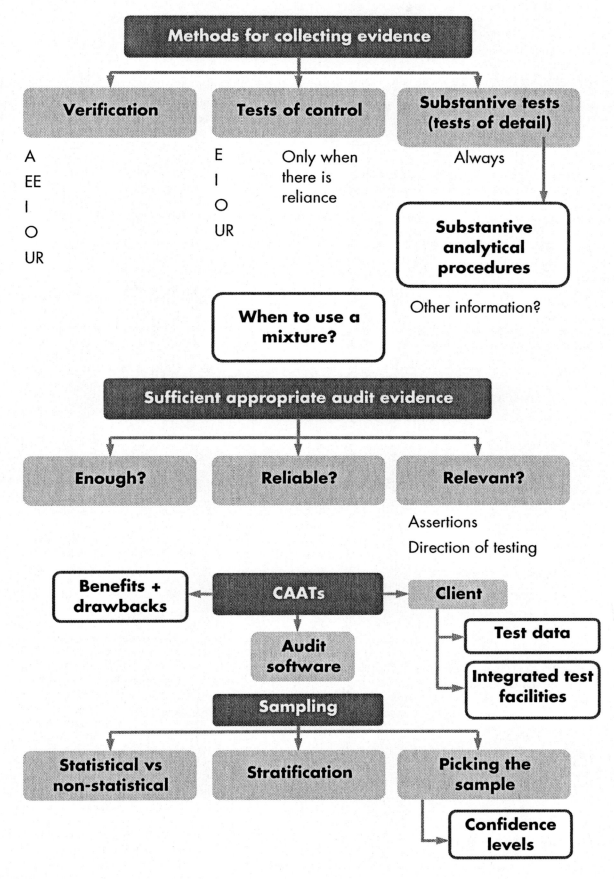

Methods for collecting evidence

Verification

A
EE
I
O
UR

Tests of control

E
I
O
UR

Only when
there is
reliance

**Substantive tests
(tests of detail)**

Always

**Substantive
analytical
procedures**

Other information?

**When to use a
mixture?**

Sufficient appropriate audit evidence

Enough?

Reliable?

Relevant?

Assertions

Direction of testing

**Benefits +
drawbacks**

CAATs

Client

**Audit
software**

Test data

**Integrated test
facilities**

Sampling

**Statistical vs
non-statistical**

Stratification

**Picking the
sample**

**Confidence
levels**

1 Methods for collecting audit evidence

In order to reach a valid opinion, you need **enough** of the **right kind** of evidence – we will consider how we determine whether we have this later, but first, let's look at the various techniques that exist in order to **collect evidence**.

1.1 Verification techniques

Auditors perform tests to obtain evidence throughout the audit, and such testing usually requires a number of **verification techniques (AEEIOUR)**:

- **A**nalytical procedures (see below)

- **E**nquiry (asking questions and confirming facts) and **E**xternal confirmation (with third parties for values or conditions)

- **I**nspection (records or other documents – sometimes called 'vouching' – as well as physical inspection of tangible assets)

- **O**bservation (of staff performing various activities)

- Recalc**U**lation (of items and amounts) or **R**e-performance (of activities and procedures)

Analytical procedures are evaluations of financial information made by a study of financial and non-financial data. They comprise the following activities:

- **Comparison** of actual with budget, across different business units or even with similar firms and industry averages. This could work for absolute amounts, percentages like profit margin or even indicators such as receivables days and should be performed across a variety of time frames.

- **Calculation** of ratios (such as net and gross margins – we will come back to these later) and **explanations** to support them (eg a 10% increase in expenditure coming from 10% more sales activity).

- **Credibility checks**, such as looking at a year's revenue for a manufacturer and dividing it by the number of working days to get a 'feel' for the implied level of daily activity, and **proof in total** (such as the relationship of payroll costs to the number of employees and their likely average pay).

A variety of methods can be used to perform these procedures, ranging from simple comparisons to complex analysis using statistics, on a company level, branch level or individual account level. The choice of procedures is a matter for the auditors' professional judgement.

Auditors are required to use analytical procedures as part of the risk assessment process at the planning stage of the audit, to:

- Identify risk areas
- Determine the nature, timing and extent of procedures

The auditor may also use analytical procedures as substantive procedures.

There are a number of factors which the auditors should consider when deciding whether to use analytical procedures as substantive procedures, such as:

- Whether the procedures are **suitable** to obtain evidence about the relevant **assertions** (given the assessed risk for those assertions)

- Whether the data the auditor is using is reliable, available and relevant

When analytical procedures identify **significant fluctuations or unexpected relationships**, the auditors must investigate by obtaining adequate explanations from management and appropriate corroborative evidence. Investigations will start with enquiries to management and then **confirmation** of management's responses.

All these verification techniques can be used in a variety of different circumstances: first, let's think about systems of internal controls and how we might test them.

1.2 Tests of control

Tests of control are tests to obtain evidence about the effective operation of the accounting and internal control systems.

In general, with the exception of analytical procedures and external confirmations, the verification techniques described above (EIOUR) can all be used to test controls.

Illustration 1: Tests of control

Consider the following examples of tests of control that could be found in a purchases system:

Audit test and description:	Working paper:	Performed by:
(1) Select a sample of 10 invoices from the Purchase Invoice Listing (PIL) and: (a) Inspect the invoice for evidence of matching to goods received note (GRN) and authorisation (b) Re-perform matching of invoice to GRN		
(2) (a) For a sample of 15 PIL totals, recalculate to batch header slip ensuring the slip is initialled. (b) Inspect batch book to ensure that all batches have been returned from the computer bureau and that any outstanding batches have been followed up.		
(3) Observe and enquire into the procedures for preparing suppliers' statement reconciliations.		
(4) Select a sample of 10 invoices from the PIL and: (a) Ensure casts and extensions have been checked (b) Re-perform casts and extensions		
(5) Select a sample of suppliers' statement reconciliations (one month in detail; review others) and re-perform these reconciliations, ensuring those statements not in agreement have been followed up.		
(6) Inspect one month's purchase ledger control account reconciliation in detail and review for other months.		
(7) Review the file of unmatched GRNs and enquire into old items still outstanding.		

Activity 1: Controls and tests – purchases

Required

Using the accounting system for purchases described for Glad Rags Limited, identify five controls and suggest tests of control that could be performed to confirm the application of each control.

Accounting systems information – Purchases

The company keeps basic stocks of all the fabric and threads required to manufacture goods from their catalogue. When stocks fall to a certain level, the stores manager requisitions a pre-set amount of that stock. There are certain fabrics that are only used for a limited number of stocks. That fabric will only be reordered if a sales order is placed for items requiring the fabric.

When the purchases department receives a requisition, they place the order with the approved supplier at a pre-arranged price. An order document is written out and kept in the orders pending file.

When the fabric or thread is received, the stores manager ensures that the quality is suitable and checks the goods against the order. The order is then passed to the accounts department and placed in the pending invoices file.

When the invoice is received, the accounts assistant, Beth Simpkins, checks the invoices against the order to ensure the price and quantity are correct and checks the VAT has been calculated correctly. She initials the invoices to show that these checks have been carried out and gives the invoice a sequence number. The invoice is then entered into the purchase ledger on the computer.

Beth prepares cheques for payment at the end of each fortnight and passes them to the director, Gladys Barton, for signature and approval. The invoices are included with the cheques as evidence of the money owed.

Most suppliers send statements at the end of the month which Beth reconciles to the purchase ledger balances. The purchase ledger control account is agreed to the total of the purchase ledger balances at the end of the month.

	Controls	**Test of controls**
(1)		
(2)		
(3)		
(4)		
(5)		

Required

Using the accounting system for payroll described for Glad Rags Limited, identify four controls and suggest tests of control that could be performed to confirm the application of each control.

Accounting systems information – Payroll

There are two payrolls, which are computerised and prepared by the director, Gladys Barton. Machining staff are paid by piece which is recorded and approved by the factory overseer, Peter Benning. Machining staff are paid weekly. Office and other administrative staff are paid a standard salary on a monthly basis.

The weekly payroll produces an exception report if machining staff are paid in excess of 20% more than their weekly average over the year. This exception report is checked back to the piece sheets which are prepared and approved by Peter Benning. Machinists are paid in cash which must be collected personally and signed for by the employee.

Monthly payments are made by automatic bank transfer from Glad Rags' bank account to the employees' bank account.

	Controls	**Test of controls**
(1)		
(2)		
(3)		
(4)		

1.3 Substantive testing

Substantive testing is audit procedures designed to detect material misstatement in the financial statements, so it includes **tests of detail** of classes of transaction, balances and disclosures, and analytical procedures.

When performing **tests of control**, if we **trust** the **controls in place within a system**, we can test them and the results of this testing will provide us with some **assurance** that the **output** of such systems can be used to produce the entity's financial statements.

Testing controls alone, however, is **not enough** to form an opinion, due to the various **limitations** of internal controls that we saw earlier. Consequently, we need

BPP
LEARNING MEDIA

to make sure that the **actual balances and amounts** themselves, which have been included in the financial statements, can be trusted (rather than the processes used to generate them). This is referred to as **substantive testing** and will **always be carried out to some extent** during an audit.

- Even if we **trusted the controls** in place, we would still use an amount of substantive testing to **supplement** this, with the extent dependent on the outcome of tests of control.

- If we could place **little or no assurance on controls** (or, in the case of a smaller entity, controls were not cost-effective) the level of substantive testing would be **increased**.

You have already seen the sort of procedures that auditors make use of when performing **both tests of control** and **substantive testing (AEIOU)** but they are sometimes **difficult** to tell apart and could form part of a question in your assessment.

Activity 3: Controls or substantive?

Required

Are each of the following audit tests a test of control or a substantive test?

Audit test		
Selection of ten invoices to test for correct authorisation in line with official signatory list		▼
Tracing ten non-current assets back to initial purchases invoices to verify their value		▼
Tracing ten non-current assets back to initial purchases invoices to verify they were allocated to the correct cost centre		▼

Picklist:

Test of control
Substantive test

1.4 Substantive analytical procedures

We saw the use of analytical procedures earlier: however, under ISA 520 *Analytical Procedures*, the auditor now has another way of performing substantive tests:

> 'The objectives of the auditor are... to obtain **relevant** and **reliable audit evidence** when using **substantive analytical procedures**.'
>
> (ISA 520: para. 3a)

What are substantive analytical procedures?

Activity 4: Ginger Ltd (1)

Ginger Ltd is a hotel chain with 10 hotels. Each hotel has 100 rooms and achieves around 55% occupancy throughout the year. The average room rate is £75 inclusive of all charges. You are the audit senior and have the draft financial statements for the year just ended.

The audit junior has been tasked with carrying out substantive analytical procedures to verify the annual revenue figure for Ginger of £15 million but is unsure whether or not he needs any other information.

Required

Is any further information required for us to verify this balance using substantive analytical procedures? Select the most appropriate option from the picklist below.

Picklist:

Bar and restaurant spend per customer	Length of stay per customer
Number of nights open during the year	No further information required

Activity 5: Ginger Ltd (2)

Required

Assume that the average room rate for Ginger Ltd is now £50 but the rest of the data is the same. Prepare extracts for reporting these findings to the audit manager, along with the implications of these findings for the audit plan.

Findings	Implications

1.5 Identifying the most appropriate mixture of tests to use

In your assessment, you are likely to be asked to determine the most appropriate mixture of tests of control and substantive testing and justify your selection. To help you with this, let's consider the following activity.

Activity 6: Mixed audit approach or substantive procedures only?

Required

For each of the following scenarios, identify the most suitable audit approach.

Scoot Ltd is a new company that has not been audited before and is dominated by its managing director and his informal operating style. Sales are of greatest importance to him as the company attempts to break into a competitive retail sector.	▼
Whitney plc is an established listed company that operates in a stable market with strong governance procedures, including an audit committee.	▼
The board of Marine Ltd has just informed its external auditor that it wishes to replace its ledger systems due to a number of errors identified in its management accounts.	▼

Substantive procedures only, with no tests of control
Tests of control and substantive procedures

---

2 Sufficient appropriate audit evidence

Consider the following from ISA 500 *Audit Evidence*:

> 'The auditor shall design and perform audit procedures that are appropriate in the circumstances for the purpose of obtaining **sufficient appropriate audit evidence**.'
>
> (ISA 500: para. 6)

What does **sufficient appropriate** audit evidence mean?

Audit evidence

Sufficiency
('enough of')

Appropriateness
('the right kind of')

Relevance

Reliability

'Sufficiency' is **subjective** and based on the auditor's **professional judgement**.

Results of **systems testing** and **assessments** of **risk** and **materiality** are used.

Additional procedures can be carried out if the auditor feels there is not enough evidence to form a valid conclusion.

Relevant evidence is judged as the right kind if it helps to **prove** a **specific characteristic** that a balance or transaction should **possess** (see below).

Reliable evidence considers the **source** of the evidence and ensures it adds **credibility** to the overall audit process (see below).

2.1 Reliable evidence

There are some generalisations about the reliability of evidence:

- It is more reliable when it is obtained from independent sources outside the entity.

- If internally generated, it is more reliable if the related controls are strong.

- If obtained directly by the auditor (rather than indirectly or by inference) then it is more reliable.

- It is more reliable when in documentary form (rather than oral).

- It is more reliable when documents are originals, not photocopies or facsimiles.

2.2 Relevant evidence – the use of assertions

Consider all the **elements** of a set of financial statements – **assets, liabilities, income, expenditure** and all their associated **disclosures**. In order to **belong there**, each part of the financial statements has to possess some **specific characteristics** (a little like **membership requirements** for a specific club or society).

The auditor needs to make sure that if something has been included in the financial statements, **it should be there** – in order to establish this, the auditor seeks evidence that is **relevant** to confirming that the element **does possess** those characteristics required in order to belong. We refer to these characteristics as **assertions.** There are two categories of assertions:

Assertions **about classes of transactions and events and related disclosures**	**Occurrence:** transactions and events that have been recorded or disclosed have occurred and pertain to the entity.
	Completeness: all transactions and events that should have been recorded have been recorded and all related disclosures that should have been included in the financial statements have been included.
	Accuracy: amounts and other data relating to recorded transactions and events have been recorded appropriately, and related disclosures have been appropriately measured and described.
	Cut-off: transactions and events have been recorded in the correct accounting period.
	Classification: transactions and events have been recorded in the proper accounts.

	Presentation: Transactions and events are appropriately aggregated or disaggregated and are clearly described, and related disclosures are relevant and understandable in the context of the requirements of the applicable financial reporting framework.
Assertions **about account balances and related disclosures** at the period-end	**Existence:** assets, liabilities, and equity interests exist. **Rights and obligations:** the entity holds or controls the rights to assets, and liabilities are the obligations of the entity. **Completeness:** all assets, liabilities and equity interests that should have been recorded have been recorded and all related disclosures that should have been included in the financial statements have been included. **Accuracy, valuation and allocation:** assets, liabilities, and equity interests are included in the financial statements at appropriate amounts and any resulting valuation or allocation adjustments are appropriately recorded and related disclosures have been appropriately measured and described. **Classification:** assets, liabilities and equity interests have been recorded in the proper accounts **Presentation:** Assets, liabilities and equity instruments are appropriately aggregated or disaggregated and are clearly described, and related disclosures are relevant and understandable in the context of the requirements of the applicable financial reporting framework.

(ISA 315: para. A124)

2.3 Direction of testing

One important matter to consider is the 'direction' of a test. When devising an audit test, it's useful to think about the two types of audit evidence available:

- **Source documents** – these include **physical assets** (such as an item of inventory or a non-current asset) and documents (ie invoices, contracts, goods despatched notes, goods received notes and timesheets)

- **Financial records** – these include the financial statements and other records which are agreed to the financial statements (ie cash books, ledgers and non-current asset registers)

If auditors are testing whether something has been **understated** in the financial statements (for example, a liability such as trade payables), they must start the test at a source document and agree the source document to the financial records. If auditors are testing whether something has been **overstated** in the financial statements (for example, non-current assets or sales revenue), they start with the financial records and trace back to source documents – to ensure the item existed in the first place.

Activity 7: Assertions (1)

Required

Consider each of the following audit tests and then select the most appropriate assertion that describes the purpose of that test.

Audit test	
Select a sample of vehicles from the list of non-current assets and obtain their certificates of ownership.	
Select a sample of receivables from the statement of financial position and agree to original invoices.	
Select a sample of receivables from the sales ledger and agree to the final amount on the statement of financial position.	
Trace a selection of payments included in cost of sales to original invoices.	

Picklist:

Existence
Rights and obligations
Cut-off
Occurrence
Completeness

Required

Consider each of the following situations and select the most appropriate audit procedure for the assertion used.

Testing cut-off for staff bonuses paid at the end of the financial year	▼
Confirming the accuracy of staff bonuses paid at the end of the financial year	▼
Confirming the value of cash investments held in a savings account by a client	▼

Picklist:

Obtaining a letter from the bank stating that a savings account is held by the client

Obtaining a letter from the bank stating the amount of savings held by the client

Reconciling payroll records to a schedule of staff bonus payments authorised by the finance director

Verifying bonus payments to payroll records to determine their timing

---

Once the testing is complete and the relevant evidence has been **collected**, as with all other outputs from the audit process, it must be **recorded** and **documented** in line with ISA 230 *Audit Documentation* (paras. 2 and 3).

3 Computer assisted audit techniques (CAATs)

Computer assisted audit techniques (CAATs) are audit techniques **carried out by the auditor** using a computer. They include **simple** procedures, such as the auditor using **spreadsheets** to manipulate data, and more **complex** computer programs and techniques, such as **embedded audit facilities** which allow the auditor continuous review of the client's system. CAATs can be **intrusive** and should only be used with **client permission**, as the client will not want the auditors' software to cause problems in his own computer systems.

Benefits of using CAATs	Drawbacks of using CAATs
This technique allows large volumes of data to be analysed at great speed, making the audit process more efficient and allowing the auditor to focus on other tasks if required.	However, like any system, they require quality data for input, otherwise the output of this process will not be reliable. Skills and experience (which may not always be available) are required to both administer and interpret the findings.

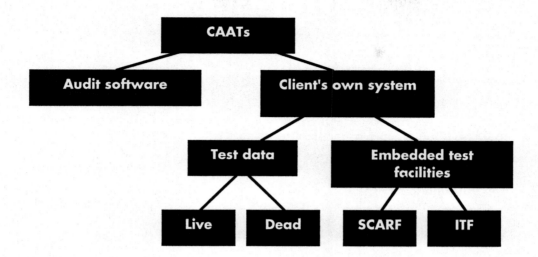

3.1 Audit software

Audit software is primarily used for **substantive testing** and suitable for the majority of audit engagements. Data will be **downloaded from the client's system to the auditor's computer** when a number of typical tests could be performed, such as:

(a) **Reperformance of calculations** eg ageing of trade receivables, casts of day books, ledger listings or inventory reports (additional comfort is gained here as the auditor's own software is being used to generate evidence)

(b) Extraction of **samples**

(c) **Analytical review** eg ratio calculations

3.2 Using the client's own system

This is primarily used for **tests of control**, and more suited to larger audit engagements. Such testing of controls will require **significant co-operation from the client**, especially in terms of computer access time. Typical uses include:

(a) **Test data** – the submission of 'dummy' data into the client's own system to ensure it is processed correctly, or not processed if the data is deliberately false. This can be conducted 'live' or **'dead'** ie as part of normal processing or at times when the computer is not in business use.

(b) **Embedded test facilities** – Systems Control and Review File (SCARF) and **integrated test facilities** (ITF) aim to extend the tests of control more fully throughout the period than test data. The former produces a **diagnostic report** of how the system is working, while the latter offers a **'virtual' copy** of the system used for testing purposes.

Activity 9: CAATs

Required

For each of the procedures listed below, select the type of CAAT which would be used to perform that procedure.

Extraction of all receivables balances older than 120 days to perform irrecoverable receivables work	▼
Input of purchases invoices with false customer numbers to ensure that the system rejects the invoices	▼
Comparison of suppliers on ledger with previous years to discover any new or missing suppliers	▼

Picklist:

Audit software
Test data

4 ISA 530 *Audit Sampling*

'The objective of the auditor, when using audit sampling, is to provide a **reasonable basis** for the auditor to draw **conclusions** about the **population** from which the sample is selected.' (ISA 530: para. 4)

Audit sampling is applying audit procedures to less than 100% of items within an account balance or class of transactions in such a way as to draw a conclusion on the account balance or class of transactions as a whole.

Statistical sampling is an approach to sampling that involves random selection of the sample items; and the use of probability theory to evaluate sample results including measurement of sampling risk (the risk of selecting a non-representative sample) (ISA 530: para. 5).

The key rule of audit sampling is that all 'sampling units' must have an equal chance of being selected for testing.

Sampling units are the individual items constituting a 'population' (account balance or class of transaction) – for example, a single receivable balance within total receivables or an individual sale within total revenue.

As you may have gathered, sampling is closely connected with risk and materiality. Sampling affects detection risk because, put simply, the more items within a population that are tested, the higher the chance of the auditor finding a misstatement.

However, if the auditor does not test every single sampling unit in the population, there is a risk that misstatements will not be detected. However carefully the sample is selected, it is possible that the sample will not be representative of the population as a whole.

Sampling, therefore, always carries a level of detection risk. The auditor has to determine an appropriate level of this risk in order to obtain the benefit of sampling (which is that auditors don't have to test everything!). The larger the sample tested, the lower the detection risk (detection risk is covered in more detail in Chapter 4).

4.1 Non-statistical sampling

Non-statistical sampling is the use of judgement to select a sample instead of a statistical technique.

In some instances, auditors will want to exercise judgement and test specific items, rather than selecting a random sample.

For instance, we have already observed that auditors should test all material items. Therefore, if the receivables' ledger contains debts that are themselves material to the financial statements, they should be selected.

This is not a statistical sample by the above definition. As these items have been selected with bias, the auditor cannot assume that they are reflective of the rest of the population, and should not project the results of testing on these items to the rest of the population. This more subjective approach, where the auditor selects samples not randomly but using his professional judgement, is called non-statistical sampling.

Another example of non-statistical sampling is where the auditor believes there is a greater risk of cut-off errors around the year end, and therefore focuses audit testing on the sales transactions just before, and just after, the year end.

4.2 Stratification

The remainder of the population should be sampled in a non-biased way. This is known as stratifying a population. **Stratification** is dividing a population into smaller sub-populations, each of which is a group of sampling units, usually by value.

Therefore, instead of testing receivables as a whole, the auditor might test two populations of receivable balances, individually material receivable balances and individually non-material receivable balances (the total of which might well be material).

In this circumstance, the auditor would not apply sampling procedures to the first population, and would instead test all of the material balances. The auditor would apply sampling procedures to the second population and select balances for testing. Results from the sampled population could be projected onto the rest of that sub-population to assess if total misstatements are likely to be material.

In the first population, there would be no need to project results because, if everything has been tested, there is nothing to project the errors against. All errors in that population should have been found.

In some audit areas, it might be more appropriate to test 100% of items, or a very high percentage of items (so that errors in the remaining balance couldn't possibly be material). An example is often additions to property, plant and equipment, where only one or two material additions may have been made in the year, and there is no need to select a sample, merely to test these items.

4.3 How to pick the sample

The important rule above comes in here. It is important that any item in the population has a chance of being picked – so, in general terms, the auditor should not bias the sample.

For example, if a company has two factories, one 20 miles from the auditor and the other 120 miles from the auditor, it is easier for the auditor to physically verify that the closer one exists. However, this would be putting an unreasonable bias on the sample selection.

In order to avoid bias, there are several common ways of selecting samples:

(1)   By **random selection**. The auditor uses a computer program or table to (mathematically) randomly select the sample.

(2)   By **systematic selection**. The auditor randomly selects the first item and then selects all the others systematically after that. For example, the auditor might pick the fifth receivable on the list of trade receivables and then every fifth or tenth after that. (This can be described as **interval sampling**.)

(3)   By **haphazard selection**. This is the approach most likely to allow audit bias to creep in. This is a method by which an auditor picks a sample with no structured technique (that is, what we would call 'at random' although human bias may reduce the mathematical randomness of the choice). It is crucial that you understand the difference between this type of sampling and 'random' sampling, outlined above.

(4)   By **Money Unit Sampling (MUS)**. This is a value-weighted selection, so (for example, in trade receivables) every nth £ is selected, rather than every nth receivable. (This is also known as interval sampling.)

(5)   By **block selection**. This involves selecting a block of continuous items (for example, April's invoices out of a population of the year's invoices). This is rarely an appropriate sample technique, as April's invoices may have different characteristics from the rest of the year and are not therefore representative of the whole population (for example, if they were posted by a different staff member due to holiday).

Activity 10: Sampling (1)

The objective of a substantive test will determine the population from which the sample is selected.

Required

For each of the objectives set out below, select the population from which the sample should be selected.

Obtain evidence that sales have not been understated		▼
Obtain evidence that sales have not been overstated		▼

Picklist:

Sales ledger
Sales order

4.4 Confidence level

When using a sample, the auditor has to be sufficiently **confident** that the results given by a sample reflect the results that would be given by testing the whole population.

Sampling, in many areas of the financial statements, is necessary because it is the only cost-effective way an audit can be performed (testing everything would take too long and be too expensive). The size of samples selected will be affected by the auditor's assessment of the **tolerable misstatement**. For tests of control, the tolerable misstatement is the maximum rate of deviation from a control that auditors are willing to accept in the population and still conclude that the preliminary assessment of control risk is valid. For tests of details (or substantive testing) the tolerable misstatement is the maximum monetary error in an account balance or class of transactions that the auditor is willing to accept and still conclude that the financial statements are true and fair.

If overall **risk of misstatement is high**, the auditor needs to be very confident that the results from a sample reflect the results that would come from the whole population. Consequently, **detection risk** needs to be reduced to an acceptably **low** level. This would **increase the size of the sample** that the auditor tests. All this is a matter of auditor judgement based on the risks of misstatements arising and materiality levels. This sort of judgement is taken at the planning stage and amended, if necessary, as the audit progresses and more facts come to light. It is taken by a senior member of the audit team and approved by the audit partner.

The auditing standard on audit sampling, ISA 530, outlines factors that impact on sample sizes, and these are summarised below.

Illustration 2: The effect of various factors on sample sizes for tests of control (ISA 530: Appendix 2)

Factor	Effect on sample size for tests of controls
Increase in extent to which auditor intends to rely on controls	**Increase** – because the more reliance the auditor intends to place on controls, the greater his assurance that they are operating effectively needs to be
Increase in the tolerable rate of deviation	**Decrease**
Increase in the expected rate of deviation	**Increase** – because if auditors expect errors to exist, they need to test more as they need to be satisfied that actual misstatement is lower than tolerable misstatement
Increase in the auditor's desired level of assurance that actual rate of deviation ≤ tolerable rate of deviation	**Increase** – because the more assurance the auditor needs, the more items he needs to test
Increase of number of sampling units	**Negligible effect**

Illustration 3: The effect of various factors on sample sizes for substantive testing (tests of detail) (ISA 530: Appendix 3)

Factor	Effect on sample size for tests of details
Increase in auditor's assessment of the risk of material misstatement	**Increase** – because the higher inherent and control risk is, the lower detection risk needs to be (hence, more tests)
Increase in the use of other procedures at the same assertion	**Decrease** – because the auditor is obtaining assurance from the other procedures (for example, analytical procedures)
Increase in the auditor's desired level of assurance that actual misstatement ≤ tolerable misstatement	**Increase** – because the more assurance the auditor needs, the more items he needs to test
Increase in tolerable misstatement	**Decrease** – because there is more chance of it being found in the sample
Increase in expected misstatement	**Increase** – because if auditors expect more errors to exist, they need to test more as they need to be satisfied that actual misstatement is lower than tolerable misstatement
Stratification of the population	**Decrease**
Number of sampling units in population	**Negligible effect**

Activity 11: Sampling (2)

Determination of sample sizes on an audit is a matter of judgement.

Required

Select the impact the following matters have on the sample sizes for tests of control.

Auditors intend to increase reliance on the company's system of internal control for the purposes of the audit.	▼
Auditors believe that there is likely to be a higher deviation rate in controls due to a new member of staff.	▼
Increased activity in the factory and new customers, resulting in 25% more sales invoices being issued during the year.	▼

Picklist:

Decrease
Increase
No effect

BPP
LEARNING MEDIA

Chapter summary

- Auditors require evidence in order to be able to form an opinion on the financial statements. This is collected using a series of different activities (AEEIOUR):
    - Analytical procedures
    - Enquiry
    - External confirmation
    - Inspection
    - Observation
    - Recalculation
    - Reperformance

- Tests of control are used to verify the operating effectiveness of accounting systems and use all the techniques listed above (AEEIOUR) apart from analytical procedures and external confirmation. They should only be used when there are suitably robust controls in place to be tested – otherwise, substantive procedures should be used instead.

- Substantive testing includes substantive analytical procedures and should always be used on an audit – however, in the absence of testing controls, an audit should be conducted on a substantive basis alone. These are also known as tests of detail.

- Auditors require sufficient (enough) appropriate (both relevant and reliable) audit evidence to form their opinion. Relevance is determined by using assertions (occurrence, completeness, accuracy, cut-off, classification/understandability, existence, rights and obligations, valuation and allocation, and presentation) and specific audit procedures must be used to test each of these.

- Computer assisted audit techniques (CAATs) are used to streamline the audit and allow for greater amounts of data to be tested with improved accuracy. They can include audit software run by the auditor and test data provided by the client.

- Sampling allows the auditor to gain assurance over large populations of data by selecting suitable samples for analysis. There are statistical and non-statistical techniques used and, in each case, care must be taken to ensure the right population is selected and the correct conclusions drawn.

- **Analytical procedures:** evaluations of financial information made by a study of financial and non-financial data

- **Assertions:** characteristics that all items within the financial statements (including disclosure notes) should possess in order to 'belong' there

- **Audit sampling:** applying audit procedures to less than 100% of items within an account balance or class of transactions in such a way as to draw a conclusion on the account balance or class of transactions as a whole

- **Audit software:** software used by the auditor to perform testing on a client's financial systems and data

- **Computer assisted audit techniques (CAATs):** audit techniques carried out by the auditor using a computer

- **Integrated test facilities:** a 'non-live' environment in a client's systems that allows real data to be processed and results investigated as part of testing

- **Non-statistical sampling:** the use of judgement to select a sample instead of a statistical technique

- **Sampling units:** the individual items constituting a 'population' (account balance or class of transaction) – for example, a single receivable balance within total receivables or an individual sale within total revenue

- **Statistical sampling:** an approach to sampling that involves random selection of the sample items; and the use of probability theory to evaluate sample results including measurement of sampling risk (the risk of selecting a non-representative sample)

- **Stratification:** dividing a population into smaller sub-populations, each of which is a group of sampling units, usually by value

- **Substantive testing:** audit procedures designed to detect material misstatement in the financial statements, so they include tests of detail of classes of transaction, balances and disclosures, and analytical procedures

- **Test data:** 'dummy' data that is fed into a client's real systems to ensure controls are operating effectively

- **Tests of control:** tests to obtain evidence about the effective operation of the accounting and internal control systems

- **Tests of detail:** another term used to describe substantive testing

- **Tolerable misstatement:** for tests of control, the maximum rate of deviation from a control that auditors are willing to accept in the population and still conclude that the preliminary assessment of control risk is valid. For tests of details (or substantive testing), the maximum monetary error in an account balance or class of transactions that the auditor is willing to accept and still conclude that the financial statements are true and fair

Test your learning

1   When designing further audit procedures as a result of risk assessment, auditors design tests which give evidence about financial statement assertions.

Select which category each assertion is relevant to.

Existence	▼
Accuracy, valuation and allocation	▼
Cut-off	▼

Picklist:

Account balances
Classes of transaction

2   Select which ONE of the following statements is the important general rule concerning audit sampling by ticking the appropriate box.

All sampling units should have an equal chance of being selected for testing. ☐

All audit areas must be subject to sampling. ☐

Auditors must always stratify a population to focus attention on high value items. ☐

The more items there are in a population, the higher the sample sizes must be. ☐

3 When using sampling techniques, auditors must select a sample such that each individual sampling unit is capable of being selected.

Select which method of sampling will be most suitable in each instance described.

Simran has been asked to select a sample of 12 sales invoices to trace from sales order to general ledger. There are 16 folders of sales orders for the year, stored in the sales office.	▼
Julie has been asked to select a sample of 5 purchase ledger accounts to carry out a supplier statement reconciliation. There are 16 purchase ledger accounts.	▼
Ben is selecting a sample of inventory lines to perform a valuation test. The audit team has been instructed to use the computerised techniques available to them, one of which is a sample selection program.	▼

Picklist:

Haphazard
Random
Systematic

4 Determination of sample sizes on an audit is a matter of judgement.

Select the impact the following matters have on the sample sizes for audit tests.

Increase in the auditor's assessment of the risk of material misstatement	▼
Increase in tolerable misstatement	▼
Decision to stratify a large population	▼

Picklist:

Decrease
Increase
No effect

5 Complete the following statement on computer assisted audit techniques.

Computer-assisted audit techniques are methods of obtaining

[_____▽] by using [_____▽].

[_____▽] is [_____▽] that can check [_____▽] on computer systems by [_____▽] or by comparing versions of [_____▽].

[_____▽] is a way of checking computer [_____▽] by inputting real or false information and observing how the program deals with it.

Picklist for line items:

Audit software
Computers
Data
Evidence
Interrogating
Programming
Programs
Software
Test data

Planning: audit risk

4

Learning outcomes

5.1	Demonstrate an understanding of how audit risk applies to external auditing
	• Components of the audit risk model, inherent, control and detection risks (sampling and non-sampling risk)
	• Relationship between the components, in particular, how auditors manage detection risk in order to keep audit risk at an acceptably low level
	• How factors such as the entity's operating environment and its system of internal control affect the assessment of inherent and control risk
	• How analytical procedures can be used to identify potential under/overstatement of items in the financial statements.
5.2	Demonstrate how the concept of materiality applies to external auditing
	• The difference between 'performance materiality' and 'materiality for the financial statements as a whole'
	• The role of materiality in planning an audit and evaluating misstatements
	• Methods used to calculate materiality thresholds
	• The difference between 'material' and 'material and pervasive'.

Assessment context

This topic supports only two tasks in the assessment but they are both significant and, in the case of audit risk, there will be multiple parts to the task. You therefore need to ensure you understand all aspects of this topic.

Qualification context

You will by now be starting to see some familiar terms such as those used by ISA 315 but this is the first time you will have seen audit risk and materiality in such detail.

Business context

The 21st century auditor needs to consider the risks associated with their chosen profession. Although this chapter focuses on overall audit risk, there are plenty of other risks that the auditor faces on a regular basis – reputation, commercial and litigation risks, to name but three.

Chapter overview

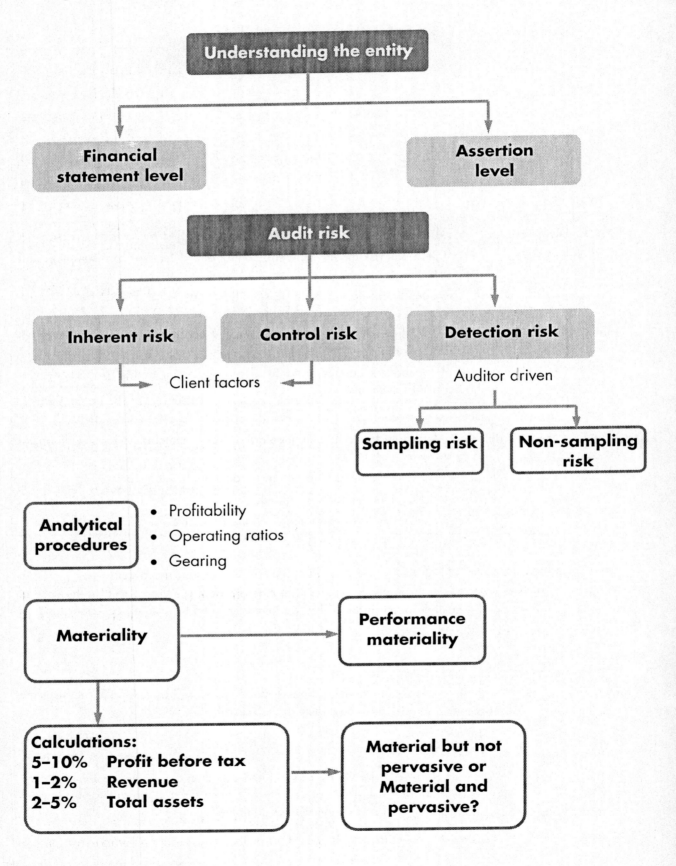

Understanding the entity

Financial statement level

Assertion level

Audit risk

Inherent risk

Control risk

Detection risk

Client factors

Auditor driven

Sampling risk

Non-sampling risk

Analytical procedures
- Profitability
- Operating ratios
- Gearing

Materiality

Performance materiality

Calculations:
5–10%   Profit before tax
1–2%   Revenue
2–5%   Total assets

Material but not pervasive or Material and pervasive?

1 Understanding the entity

We have already seen how ISA 315 *Identifying and Assessing the Risks of Material Misstatement through Understanding of the Entity and its Environment* provides guidance on systems and controls but, in addition to this, it defines some key terminology that the auditor needs in order to plan the forthcoming external audit:

> '**Risk assessment procedures** – The audit procedures performed to obtain an **understanding of the entity** and its environment, including the entity's internal control, to identify and assess the **risks of material misstatement**, whether due to fraud or error, at the financial statement and assertion level.'
>
> (ISA 315: para. 4d)

Understanding the entity and its environment helps to prepare the auditor by planning the audit effectively to deliver a valid opinion.

Such an opinion is fraught with uncertainty, however, and auditors need to plan for possible cases of fraud or error jeopardising the truth and fairness of the financial statements which they might not detect.

The extract from ISA 315 mentions risks at **two levels**, each of which could influence the opinion given by the auditor:

- The **financial statement level** – there is a possibility that certain factors might have a detrimental effect on the **whole set of financial statements**. For example, flaws in the control environment, an overall lack of management integrity or competence or even **adverse economic conditions** could lead to the entire set of statements being affected.

- The **assertion level** – there may only be **one specific element** of the financial statements that is at risk of material misstatement due to problems with one or more **characteristics** of that element. For example, if **material assets** listed on the statement of financial position are **incorrectly valued**, there is a **material misstatement** in respect of them due to the **assertions made by management about their value**. We will look at assertions in more detail later.

ISA 315 (Revised) (Appendix 1) goes on to list the circumstances that should be considered as part of an entity's risk assessment process:

- Changes in the operating environment (regulatory or even competitive)
- New personnel within an organisation
- New or revamped information systems
- Rapid growth
- New technology
- New business models, products or activities
- Corporate restructurings
- Expanded foreign operations
- New accounting pronouncements

The external auditor therefore faces a **serious problem** when agreeing to deliver an audit opinion – in the same way as any **critic** might be at risk when asked for their opinion, this could easily be **discredited** if it has not taken into consideration all **available information** and the auditor's **expertise**. How does the auditor make sure such **information** and **expertise** has been taken into consideration? The answer lies in **understanding the risks** faced by auditors and **working to control them** by use of the **audit risk model**.

2 Audit risk

This is the risk that the auditor **does not detect** one or more of the risks that relate to an audit and gives an opinion that the financial statements are **true and fair** when, in reality, they are materially misstated in some way, due to **incorrect** and/or **inappropriate accounting** or **disclosure**. It is a factor of **inherent risk**, **control risk** and **detection risk**.

2.1 The audit risk model

The model works by **isolating** elements of the audit process and reviewing each one to see what the impact on audit work will be. The various elements are as follows:

> **Audit Risk = Inherent Risk × Control Risk × Detection Risk**

Audit risk

This is the risk that you give an **incorrect opinion** – for example, the auditor may wish to limit the chance of this happening to only **5%** (ie working towards **95% accuracy**)

Inherent risk

Such risk is always present in areas of the **client** that are **susceptible** or prone to fraud or error (such as high staff turnover, cash transactions, complex calculations, high value items or those requiring estimation or judgement)

Control risk

This is another risk only ever present at **clients**, representing the risk of controls not preventing or detecting fraud or error (eg human error or management override)

Where does **detection risk** come into the formula then?

> **Detection risk is the risk that audit procedures will not detect a misstatement.** It is a **representation** of the **acceptable amount of risk** faced by the auditor. As inherent and control risk increase, the level of **acceptable detection risk decreases** and the auditor therefore performs more testing to **keep audit risk** at an **acceptable level**.

During the process of testing to address detection risk, sampling (which you have already covered) will be used frequently – however, this exposes the auditor to two types of detection risk that you need to know about – sampling risk and non-sampling risk:

- **Sampling risk** – this is the risk that occurs every time a sample is selected and represents the risk that the sample does not adequately represent the population.

- **Non-sampling risk** – this is subtly different from sampling risk and occurs from poor interpretation of a sample by the auditor: for example, the auditor may have limited experience of sampling and may have selected a suitable sample, but fails to derive the right conclusions from the data obtained (this may occur if the auditor is short of time or does not fully understand the client).

In general terms, the audit risk model could be looked at as a **mathematical equation** where you are looking for the **balancing figure**. Detection risk does just that by considering the **desired audit risk** and the likely **inherent** and **control risks** posed by the client – the auditor then has to consider the amount of work that needs to be done to balance the equation.

Activity 1: Detection risk

You are the auditor of J Club Ltd and are working out how much work you need to do to stay within your 95% accuracy figure that you use in your firm's marketing literature.

Required

Show how much 'detective work' you will need to do in each of the following two scenarios if J Club Ltd has risks, as follows:

(i)   Inherent risk =   50%   Control risk = 20%

(ii)   Inherent risk =   50%   Control risk = 40%

Scenario (i)   Scenario (ii)

Detection risk =   Detection risk =

Activity 2: Audit risk

Required

Select whether the following statements in respect of audit risk are true or false.

If inherent and control risk have been determined to be high, auditors will have to carry out a high level of detailed testing to render overall audit risk acceptable.	▼
The head of internal audit has just been suspended from one of your clients on suspicion of fraud. As a result, you assess that control risk has fallen.	▼
One of your largest retail clients has decided to cease taking cash at all its stores. You assess that inherent risk will fall for that client.	▼

Picklist:

True

False

3 Analytical procedures and audit risk

Much of the evidence gathering that the auditor does is based on the verification techniques outlined earlier in the course (**AEEIOUR**) and the **first** of these – **analytical procedures** – is based on the auditor's ability to **interpret financial information**.

At the **risk assessment stage** of the audit, **ISA 315** helps to identify aspects of the entity being audited that the auditor might not have been aware of, using analytical procedures to identify **plausible relationships** between items of **financial** and **non-financial information** (ISA 315: para. 6(b)). Broadly speaking, **assets** should not be **overstated** nor **liabilities understated** when supported by relevant data (such as revenues or purchases). Examples of the **type of relationships** sought could include:

- Consistent amounts of non-current assets, working capital and expenditure for a specific level of activity (eg consistent receivables and revenues increases)

- Consistent lengths of time taken to collect debts or pay invoices

- Consistent amounts of return for a given amount of investment in non-current assets

- Consistent amounts of debt to equity

The amount of consistency in all these areas is assessed over a **number of time frames** to allow the auditor to **pinpoint** any **specific areas** of **risk**. There are a number of important accounting ratios that could be used for this:

Gross profit	$\dfrac{\text{Gross profit}}{\text{Revenue}} \times 100\%$
This should be calculated in total and by product, area and month/quarter if possible.	
Receivables turnover period	$\dfrac{\text{Receivables}}{\text{Revenue}} \times 365$
Inventory turnover ratio	$\dfrac{\text{Cost of sales}}{\text{Inventory}}$
Current ratio	$\dfrac{\text{Current assets}}{\text{Current liabilities}}$
Quick or acid test ratio	$\dfrac{\text{Current assets (excluding inventory)}}{\text{Current liabilities}}$
Gearing ratio	$\dfrac{\text{Loans}}{\text{Share capital and reserves}} \times 100\%$
Return on capital employed	$\dfrac{\text{Profit before tax}}{\text{Total assets} - \text{Current liabilities}}$

You should be familiar with these ratios from your other studies. Remember that ratios mean very little when used in isolation. They should be **calculated for previous periods** and for **comparable companies**. Audit working papers should contain summarised accounts and the chosen ratios for prior years. In addition to looking at the more usual ratios, the auditors should consider examining **other ratios** that may be **relevant** to the particular **client's business**, such as revenue per passenger mile for an airline operator client, or fees per partner for a professional office.

One further important technique is to examine **important related accounts** in conjunction with each other. It is often the case that revenue and expense accounts are related to statement of financial position accounts and comparisons should be made to ensure that the relationships are reasonable.

Activity 3: IZK Ltd

Required

Use analytical procedures to determine four balances from IZK Ltd that you would investigate further for risk of material misstatement – select your answers from the picklist below.

IZK Ltd
Statement of financial position as at 30 September 20X6

	20X6 £	20X5 £
ASSETS		
Non-current assets		
Property, plant and equipment	46,595	41,675
Current assets		
Inventories	60,120	58,675
Trade and other receivables	140,674	124,968
Cash and cash equivalents	17,547	6,617
	218,341	190,260
Total assets	264,936	231,935
EQUITY AND LIABILITIES		
Equity		
Share capital	1,000	1,000
Retained earnings	184,187	142,039
	185,187	143,039
Non-current liabilities		
Bank loans	4,762	14,910
Current liabilities		
Trade and other payables	74,987	73,986
Total liabilities	79,749	88,896
Total equity and liabilities	264,936	231,935

Picklist:

Bank loans
Cash and cash equivalents
Property, plant and equipment
Retained earnings
Share capital
Trade and other payables
Trade and other receivables

Activity 4: Bucket Ltd

The external auditor is required to undertake analytical procedures as part of the planning process in order to identify and evaluate the risks of material misstatement of figures in the financial statements. The results of the analytical procedures conducted on trade receivables and trade payables in the financial statements of an audit client are shown below.

Required

Select whether the results indicate that trade receivables and trade payables at Bucket Ltd may have been under- or overstated.

The results show that, compared with the previous year:

Trade receivables have increased by 25% and revenue has increased by 7%	▼
Trade payables have decreased by 5% and purchases has increased by 4%	▼

Picklist:

Overstated
Understated

4 Materiality

If either the **omission** or **misstatement** of an item could reasonably affect the economic decisions of users of a set of financial statements, then that item is considered **material** to those financial statements.

We are familiar with the term 'material misstatement' but we have not yet defined the term 'material'. ISA 320 *Materiality in Planning and Performing an Audit* helps us with this:

'When establishing the overall audit strategy, the auditor shall determine **materiality** for the financial statements as a whole. If, in the specific circumstances of the entity, there is one or more particular **classes of transactions, account balances or disclosures** for which misstatements of lesser amounts than materiality for the financial statements as a whole could **reasonably be expected to influence the economic decisions of users taken on the basis of the financial statements**, the auditor shall also determine the materiality level or levels to be applied to those particular classes of transactions, account balances or disclosures.'

(ISA 320: para. 10)

Items can be material by nature: **related parties** and **related party transactions** are considered to be a significant risk because they affect profits earned but may not be obvious to the audit team – hence they should always be prioritised and reported to senior audit team members to ensure correct treatment in the financial statements.

Materiality is important as it **determines** the threshold above which **further audit work** becomes necessary, as well as confirming those **misstatements** or **omissions** that will have to be **considered as part of the audit opinion**.

4.1 Calculation of materiality

The auditor must calculate a suitable level of materiality for the financial statements as a whole. This will often be a percentage of a significant benchmark in the financial statements.

Calculating materiality will always be a matter of professional judgement, so these percentages will not simply be applied without thought, but a useful guide to materiality levels is to consider that something is material if it is:

- 5–10% of profit before tax
- 1–2% of revenue
- 2–5% of total assets

The auditor may need to calculate material levels for specific items in financial statements which are particularly significant to users for any reason. Some items might be material simply because of what they are. Due to the legal restrictions around directors' remuneration disclosures in the UK, any matter relating to directors in financial statements is usually considered to be material.

In addition, a misstatement might be considered material because of its effect. For example, if a small misstatement made the company breach a covenant made with its bank, it might be considered material.

Activity 5: Material or not?

Profit is £100,000 and materiality has been set at 5% of profit.

Required

Select whether the following items are likely to be considered material or not material.

There is misstatement in receivables, value £7,500.	▼
A loan to a director has been disclosed in the financial statement at £2,000. Actually the correct sum is £2,010.	▼
The company is required to keep a current asset ratio of 2:1. A misstatement of £100 has been found in receivables, which will cause the ratio to drop below this level.	▼

Picklist:

Material
Not material

4.2 Performance materiality

Performance materiality is the amount or amounts set by the auditor at less than materiality for the financial statements as a whole. This reduces to an appropriately low level the probability that the aggregate of uncorrected and undetected misstatements exceeds materiality for the financial statements as a whole.

> 'The auditor shall determine **performance materiality** for purposes of assessing the risks of material misstatement and **determining** the **nature**, **timing** and **extent** of **further audit procedures**.'
>
> (ISA 320: para. 11)

Setting one level of materiality means that there could be items **below** this level which are misstated but not classed as material and hence not tested – if there were several of these, there is a risk that the sum of these could constitute a material misstatement that the auditor never knew about.

To address this risk, a **second** level of materiality is set by the auditor and used to select specific amounts where the risk of **aggregate immaterial misstatements** is highest. It is again a matter of **professional judgement** for the auditor on both the **amount** and the **classes of transaction** or **account balance** selected. This is called **'performance materiality'**. You will explore this idea further when considering **ISA 450 *Evaluation of Misstatements Identified During the Audit***.

4.3 Revision of materiality as the audit progresses

'The auditor shall **revise materiality** for the financial statements as a whole (and, if applicable, the materiality level or levels for particular classes of transactions, account balances or disclosures) in the event of **becoming aware of information during the audit** that would have caused the auditor to have determined a **different amount (or amounts) initially**.' (ISA 320: para. 12)

'If the auditor concludes that a **lower materiality** for the financial statements as a whole (and, if applicable, materiality level or levels for particular classes of transactions, account balances or disclosures) **than that initially determined is appropriate**, the auditor shall determine whether it is necessary to **revise performance materiality**, and whether the **nature, timing and extent of the further audit procedures remain appropriate**.'

(ISA 320: para. 13)

4.4 Documentation

'The auditor shall include in the audit documentation the following amounts and the factors considered in their determination:

(a) Materiality for the financial statements as a whole

(b) If applicable, the materiality level or levels for particular classes of transactions, account balances or disclosures

(c) Performance materiality

(d) Any revision of (a)-(c) as the audit progressed.'

(ISA 320: para. 14)

It is logical that, in order to **document** the process of reaching the audit opinion, as well as the assumptions made, any **changes** in those assumptions should also be documented.

BPP
LEARNING MEDIA

4.5 'Material' or 'material and pervasive'?

You may be asked to differentiate between the terms 'material' and 'material and pervasive' when evaluating the materiality of a misstatement or similar issue. From **ISA 705 (revised)** *Modifications to the Opinion in the Independent Auditor's Report*, the term **'material and pervasive'** has the following **definitions**:

- Are **not confined** to **specific elements**, accounts or items of the financial statements

- If so confined, represent or could represent a **substantial proportion** of the financial statements

- In relation to disclosures, are **fundamental** to users' understanding of the financial statements (ISA 705: para. 5(a)).

Activity 6: Materiality issues

Required

Select whether the following statements in respect of materiality are true or false.

Performance materiality should be set at less than materiality for the financial statements as a whole.	▼
Materiality is a measure of the importance of items to a reader of financial statements.	▼
Items may be material due to their size, nature or effect on the financial statements.	▼
A building carried in the financial statements is judged to be 'material and pervasive' if it represents 70% of total assets and 150% of profit before tax and is subject to an impairment review due to extensive damage. It is the only premises of a trading company that cannot relocate due to commercial pressure.	▼

Picklist:

True

False

- Auditors start to evaluate the planning process by attempting to understand the entity that is being audited, both at the financial statement level (risks that affect the whole financial statements) and at the assertion level (more specific issues related to the way that certain amounts are carried within the financial statements).

- Risk assessment procedures require an understanding of the factors that go into creating audit risk:

  - Inherent risk – the susceptibility of certain things being misstated (this is client-driven).

  - Control risk – the inability of systems of internal control to deal with such inherent risks (this is also client-driven).

  - Detection risk – the risk that the auditor does not do enough testing to take account of inherent and control risk. This is auditor-driven and includes sampling risk (the risk that a sample is not representative of the population) and non-sampling risk (the risk that results of testing are misinterpreted).

- Analytical procedures are used to identify and understand risks within a set of financial statements and use techniques such as ratios, comparisons and other techniques to understand profitability, operating and gearing issues presented by an audited entity.

- Materiality is the term used to describe the significance of certain items within the financial statements depending on the importance placed upon them by users of those financial statements. It can be assessed numerically (such as a percentage of profit before tax or total assets) but also qualitatively (by nature, such as a related party transaction). Items can be assessed as not just 'material' but also 'material and pervasive' if they meet certain criteria relating to their size and impact which auditors also need to consider.

- Performance materiality is an amount set at below materiality to allow the auditor to test for items where, in the auditor's judgement, there may be misstatements that are individually immaterial but in aggregate, they could represent a material misstatement.

- Materiality is one of the single most difficult areas for the auditor due to the heavy reliance on judgement to make it work effectively.

Keywords

- **Audit risk:** the risk that the auditor does not detect one or more of the risks that relate to an audit and gives an opinion that the financial statements are true and fair when, in reality, they are materially misstated in some way, due to incorrect and/or inappropriate accounting or disclosure. It is a factor of inherent risk, control risk and detection risk

- **Control risk:** another risk only ever present at clients, representing the risk of controls not preventing or detecting fraud or error (eg human error or management override)

- **Detection risk:** the risk that audit procedures will not detect a misstatement. It is a representation of the acceptable amount of risk faced by the auditor. As inherent and control risk increase, the level of acceptable detection risk decreases and the auditor therefore performs more testing to keep audit risk at an acceptable level

- **Inherent risk:** Such risk is always present in areas of the client that are susceptible or prone to fraud or error (such as high staff turnover, cash transactions, complex calculations, high value items or those requiring estimation or judgement)

- **Material and pervasive:**
  - Are not confined to specific elements, accounts or items of the financial statements
  - If so confined, represent or could represent a substantial proportion of the financial statements
  - In relation to disclosures, are fundamental to users' understanding of the financial statements

- **Materiality:** if either the omission or misstatement of an item could reasonably affect the economic decisions of users of a set of financial statements, then that item is considered material to those financial statements

- **Non-sampling risk:** subtly different from sampling risk and occurs from poor interpretation of a sample by the auditor: for example, the auditor may have limited experience of sampling and may have selected a suitable sample, but fails to derive the right conclusions from the data obtained (this may occur if the auditor is short of time or does not fully understand the client)

- **Performance materiality:** the amount or amounts set by the auditor at less than materiality for the financial statements as a whole. This reduces to an appropriately low level the probability that the aggregate of uncorrected and undetected misstatements exceeds materiality for the financial statements as a whole

- **Sampling risk:** the risk that occurs every time a sample is selected and represents the risk that the sample does not adequately represent the population

1   Complete the statement.

The auditors must gain an understanding of the following areas of a business:

....

....

....

....

....

2   Select which ONE of the following statements best summarises why auditors must gain an understanding of the entity using the appropriate tick box.

In order to understand internal control systems   ☐

In order to be able to assess risks   ☐

In order to see what items there are to be audited   ☐

In order to eliminate items from testing   ☐

3   Complete the definitions using the items in the picklist below.

[_____ ▼] risk is the risk that the auditors give an [_____ ▼] opinion on the financial statements.

[_____ ▼] risk is the risk that the entity's internal control system will not prevent or detect and correct errors.

[_____ ▼] risk is the risk that items will be misstated due to their [_____ ▼] or due to their [_____ ▼].

[_____ ▼] risk is the risk that misstatements will exist in financial statements and the auditors will not discover them.

Picklist for line items:

Audit
Context
Control
Detection
Inappropriate
Incorrect
Inherent
Nature

4   Select whether the following statements concerning audit risks are true or false.

Auditors cannot affect inherent and control risk as inherent and control risks are the risks that errors will arise in the financial statements as a result of control problems or the nature of items in the financial statements of the entity. The auditors cannot control those factors.	▼
If inherent and control risk are high, detection risk should be rendered low to come to an overall acceptable level of risk. In order for detection risk to be low, the auditors will have to carry out a lower level of testing.	▼

Picklist:

True
False

5   When planning an audit of financial statements, the auditor is required to consider how factors such as the entity's operating environment and its system of control affect the risk of material misstatement in the financial statements.

Select whether the following factors are likely to increase or reduce the risk of misstatement.

The control environment is weak and there is considerable pressure on management to improve results year on year.	▼
Management has implemented improvements in controls as a result of weaknesses identified last year.	▼

Picklist:

Increase
Reduce

6   Select whether the following statements in respect of materiality are true or false.

Materiality is the concept of significance to users of the financial statements.	▼
Performance materiality will usually be higher than materiality assessed for the financial statements as a whole.	▼

Picklist:

True
False

7   When planning an audit of financial statements, the auditor is required to consider how factors such as the entity's nature and operating environment affect the risk of material misstatement in the financial statements.

Select whether the following factors are likely to increase or reduce the risk of misstatement.

The company has diversified its operations during the year.	▼
The company has discontinued operations in its riskiest operating area during the year.	▼

Picklist:

Increase
Reduce

Planning: audit procedures

5

Learning outcomes

5.3	Analyse the key audit risks for a given situation
	• Analyse factors relating to a given audited entity's operating environment and system of internal control give rise to risk of material misstatement in the financial statements.
5.4	Apply audit procedures to achieve audit objectives
	• Develop procedures to obtain sufficient appropriate evidence in respect of the relevant assertions for key figures in the financial statements, in particular
	– Non-current assets – Inventory – Receivables – Cash and bank – Borrowings – Payables – Provisions – Revenue – Payroll and other expenses – Accruals and prepayments.

Assessment context

Although there are only two learning outcomes listed here (and therefore only two tasks in your assessment), they are both written tasks and will each be worth 10 marks, so this topic is essential for you to engage with.

Qualification context

Most of this chapter will be application of terms previously seen in your AAT studies, although the use of some terms may not initially be clear. Try to refer to previous units if there are elements of terminology that you are unfamiliar with.

Business context

Inventory and work in progress (WIP) often represent a significant asset on the statement of financial position, with the value of inventory also having a direct impact on profit. A considerable amount of audit effort is usually devoted to this area because of these factors – talk to any seasoned audit professional and they will usually have the most engaging stories to tell about either the nature of an inventory count (eg smoked haddock stored in a cold, draughty shed) or the timing (eg 6am on New Year's Day!).

The audit of other assets is often a major part of the audit for an audit firm, as it usually requires significant work on valuation and existence to counter the risk of overstated amounts. Given the nature of the agency problem that we saw in the first topic, it is entirely possible that the directors of an entity may try to make their company seem as big as possible, meaning that auditors will usually have their work cut out for them.

The audit of liabilities is quite a change for the auditor – instead of being on the lookout for overstated assets used to bolster a potentially fragile statement of financial position, you are now faced with the possibility of items being either understated or even ignored. Remember that visibility (or rather lack of it) is the biggest audit risk here – the collapse of the Enron Company in 2001 was partly due to hidden off balance sheet financing.

Chapter overview

Audit risk

Factors that increase or decrease the risk of material misstatement within the financial statements

Audit procedures

Written task

Non-current assets

- Capital items
- Leases

Inventory

- Inventory count
- Raw materials
- WIP
- Finished goods
- Cut-off

Receivables

- Circularisation

Cash and bank

- Bank reconciliation
- Bank letter

Borrowings

- Amounts
- Disclosures

Payables

- Completeness
- Valuation

Provision

- Judgement

Revenue

- Double entry

Payroll

- Completeness
- Existence

Purchases

- Occurrence

Accruals

Prepayments

**Bills
Insurance
Expenses**

1 Audit risk analysis for a given situation

We've already seen how the auditor can use the various elements of the audit risk model (inherent risk, control risk and detection risk) to understand the risks presented by an audit client. However, you are likely to be asked to complete a written task within the assessment where you identify areas of audit risk from a given set of circumstances in a scenario.

Activity 1: Risk of misstatement

When planning an audit of financial statements, the external auditor is required to consider how factors such as the entity's operating environment and its system of internal control affect the risk of misstatement in the financial statements.

Required

Select whether the following factors are likely to increase or reduce the risk of misstatement.

The entity is to be sold and the purchase consideration will be determined as a multiple of reported profit.	▼
The company has a history of being slow to follow new accounting standards and guidance.	▼

Picklist:

Increase
Reduce

Activity 2: Pebbles Ltd

Pebbles Ltd is a private limited company which owns a number of fish and chip shops in seaside resorts on the south coast.

The owners of the company are Mark O'Neill and John White. They each own 50% of the share capital and are both directors. John is responsible for the financial side of the business. He is thinking of selling his stake in the company but wants to wait until the audited accounts are available.

The trade is very seasonal, with high turnover and profits in the summer. However, the restaurants remain open throughout the year as they make sales to weekend and Christmas holidaymakers.

All sales are made on a cash basis. Purchases are made on credit from a number of suppliers. Stocks (inventory) are kept in refrigerators on the premises and have to be used within one week of purchase.

During the summer months, a large number of casual workers are employed. Many are at school or college and are taking a holiday job. Some only last a few days and are never seen again! During the rest of the year, there are around 30 people on the payroll. This element of the workforce is fairly stable.

The company owns some of the premises from which the business is run. Others are leased.

Identify and describe FOUR factors from the scenario that could increase the risk of misstatement in the financial statements of Pebbles Ltd.

(1)

(2)

(3)

(4)

---

2 Audit procedures

When using **substantive procedures** to test the various items on the statement of financial position, the auditor considers the **appropriate assertions** for these balances as they help auditors to gather **evidence** in order to form a **conclusion** about each specific item.

2.1 Non-current assets

Non-current assets are assets held for continuing use in the business.

We saw from earlier chapters that, for **assets** and **liabilities**, the relevant assertions are:

- Existence
- Completeness
- Rights and obligations (or ownership)
- Valuation
- Disclosure (or description)

We will now look at other items that are classified as either **assets** or **debit balances** (usually both, but not always). First is the asset balance that is usually the largest for an entity: **non-current assets**. **Inventory**, one important area of the audit, is covered in detail in section 2.2 of this chapter.

An important test when reviewing non-current assets is to ensure that only **capital expenditure** is included on the statement of financial position.

Activity 3: JICS driving school

You are the audit senior working on the audit of JICS driving school. You are testing non-current assets for overstatement (existence). Based on your review of the non-current assets register, you have noted that it includes the items listed below.

Required

Identify four items from the picklist that you do not believe to be capital in nature.

Picklist:

10 × Ford Fiestas
2 × PCs and monitors for the office
2 × desk telephones
10 × mobile telephones
Car insurance
Car servicing
Installation of dual controls in cars
Replacement tyre for car no. 6
Repairs to bumper of car no. 4
Office fixtures and fittings
'JICS' signs to go on top of cars

Activity 4: Campey Ltd non-current assets

Below is a schedule of non-current assets at Campey Ltd.

Required

Set out, in a manner suitable for inclusion in the audit plan, the audit procedures to be undertaken for each assertion in order to ensure that non-current assets are fairly stated in the financial statements. You have already verified the opening balances to the prior year audit file.

	Land £	Buildings £	Vehicles £	Fittings £	Total £
Cost at 1 October 20X8	1,000,000	3,500,000	60,000	125,150	4,685,150
Additions	–	–	15,000	800	15,800
Disposals	–	–	–	–	–
Cost at 30 November 20X9	1,000,000	3,500,000	75,000	125,950	4,700,950
Accumulated depreciation at 1 October 20X8		140,000	26,250	37,545	203,795
Depreciation charge	–	70,000	12,188	18,893	101,081
Accumulated depreciation at 30 November 20X9	–	210,000	38,438	56,438	304,876
Carrying amount at 30 November 20X9	1,000,000	3,290,000	36,562	69,512	4,396,074
Carrying amount at 1 October 20X8	1,000,000	3,360,000	33,750	87,605	4,481,355

Note. Depreciation rates are 2% straight line for buildings, 25% diminishing balance for vehicles and 15% straight line for fittings.

Completeness

Rights and obligations

Existence

Valuation

Leases (IAS 17)

Leases are studied in the Level 4 *Financial Statements of Limited Companies* unit. You do not need detailed knowledge of the financial reporting standard *Leases* (IAS 17) for the *External Auditing* unit. However, you need to understand the key risk associated with this item – which is that it may be incorrectly included on the statement of financial position or statement of profit or loss.

A lease is a contract between a lessor and a lessee for the hire of a specific asset.

IAS 17 (para. 10) requires companies to account for leases in accordance with the commercial reality (substance) of the arrangement, rather than its legal form.

Legal form	The lessor retains ownership of the asset
Substance of the arrangement	The lessee has the right to use the asset for an agreed period of time, in return for rental payments

Finance lease – definition

A **finance lease** is a lease that transfers **substantially all the risks and rewards of ownership** of an asset to the lessee. Title may or may not be eventually transferred.

IAS 17 identifies five situations that would normally lead to a lease being classified as a finance lease.

- The lease **transfers ownership** of the asset to the lessee at the end of the lease term.

- The lessee has the **option to purchase** the asset at a price sufficiently below fair value at exercise date, that it is **reasonably certain** the option will be exercised.

- The lease term is for a **major part** of the asset's economic life, even if title is not transferred.

- Present value of minimum lease payments (PVMLP) amounts to substantially all of the asset's fair value at inception.

- The leased asset is so specialised that only the lessee can use it without major modifications.

Essentially, under a finance lease, the lease is really a loan for the sum of money the lessee would need to buy the asset outright (IAS 17: para. 10).

Where an item is acquired under a finance lease, the financial statements will show:

Illustration 1: Finance leases disclosure in the financial statements of lessees (IAS 17: paras. 20, 25 and 27)

Under a finance lease, the financial statements will show:

Statement of financial position (extract)

	£
Non-current assets	
Property, plant and equipment	X
Non-current liabilities	
Lease liability	X
Current liabilities	
Lease liability	<u>X</u>
	<u>X</u>

Statement of profit or loss and other comprehensive income (extract)	
	£
Depreciation charge (in relevant expense category)	X
Finance charges	X

Operating lease

An **operating lease** is a lease other than a finance lease.

With an operating lease, lease payments are recognised as an expense in the statement of profit or loss and other comprehensive income on a straight line basis over the lease term (IAS 17: para. 33).

Audit risk for leases

The auditors must test leased items to verify that they are correctly accounted for as a finance lease or operating lease.

2.2 Inventory

The audit approach for **inventory** must include the three main elements of inventory balances seen in the statement of financial position: **quantity**, **valuation**, and **disclosure**.

One audit test in particular gives evidence in relation to **completeness, rights and obligations** (ie ownership) and **existence**. This test is **attending the physical inventory count** carried out by the entity being audited and it provides evidence of inventory **quantity**. It can also provide **corroborative evidence** of the likely **valuation** of such an asset due to recording information about the **condition** of inventory as well.

There are **three methods** for an entity to physically count its inventory:

- Year end count, where the entire inventory of the entity is counted as close to the reporting period end as possible to provide a figure for the closing inventory balance

- Interim count with follow through to year end – as above, but the count occurs during the year and all items both inwards and outwards are reconciled to arrive at a calculated amount

- Continuous inventory records and perpetual inventory – an automated system records all items inwards and outwards, and maintains an ongoing balance of inventory at any one time – this is tested periodically as part of the entity's normal controls assessment

The auditor will attend the entity's physical inventory count to verify inventory quantities but **it is not the auditor's responsibility to count the inventory**.

This is carried out as part of the legal responsibilities of the management of the entity to keep accounting records in line with the **Companies Act 2006**.

Quantity

The **most common method** for the auditor to gain evidence as to the **amount** of inventory held at the end of the reporting period is to **attend** the year end inventory count.

Activity 5: Paper Products Ltd

You are the senior on the audit of Paper Products Ltd. Your client imports paper from Scandinavia and supplies it to major publishers and stationery suppliers in the UK. A new team member will be attending the annual inventory count this Saturday. It is your responsibility to brief him on how he should prepare for the count and what he should do when he is there.

Required

List the points you will cover during your briefing with the new team member.

Before:

During:

After:

Activity 6: Inventory assertions

Required

Consider each of the following tests plus results from the audit file recording attendance at the annual inventory count of Glad Rags. From the list of assertions supplied, select the most appropriate assertion for that test.

Test **Form an opinion of the condition of inventory and record any instances of damage or obsolescence.** **Result** There were 15 × 10m rolls of fabric stored near the roof of the warehouse where birds had nested, making the fabric unusable.	▼
Test **Trace 10 × 10m rolls of fabric from the inventory sheets to the relevant shelves of the warehouse.** **Result** All 10 rolls were found on the shelves in the locations specified by the main accounting system.	▼
Test **Trace 10 × 10m rolls of fabric from the relevant shelves of the warehouse to the inventory sheets.** **Result** All 10 rolls were traced back to the list generated by the main accounting system.	▼

Test

Confirm that the fabric and garments held in the secure off-site storage facility are to be included in Glad Rags' inventory balance by verifying them to supporting documentation and invoices.

Result

All rolls of fabric and garments were traced back to storage invoices and haulage records, confirming that they belong to Glad Rags.

Picklist:

Completeness
Rights and obligations
Existence
Valuation

Valuation

Once quantity is established by attending the entity's count, the next characteristic of inventory must be assessed – **valuation**. Inventory must be valued at the **lower** of **cost** and **net realisable value (NRV)** in order to comply with IAS 2 *Inventories* (para. 9). The auditor will therefore need to design procedures that establish amounts for each for this comparison to occur.

Activity 7: Valuing inventory

Your firm is the external auditor of William Ltd. William Ltd owns a grocery store in a small town. You are responsible for planning the procedures to be undertaken to test the valuation of inventories in the financial statements for the year ended 31 March 20X4. An inventory listing will be prepared as at 31 March 20X4, listing the products held at the year end, the number of each type of product and their cost.

Required

Set out, in a manner suitable for inclusion in the audit plan, the audit procedures to be undertaken to test the valuation of the inventory figure in the financial statements for the year ended 31 March 20X4.

Note. You do not need to discuss audit procedures undertaken at the year end in relation to the inventory count.

Other audit tests for inventory

We saw the use of **accounting estimates** mentioned in the solution to the previous activity when discussing the possible impact on the NRV of supermarket inventory of items going literally **'past their shelf life'**. Such a loss requires a degree of **judgement** by the entity's management and the auditor needs to establish whether their conclusion is **reasonable** or not. Similar estimates are also required for valuing items of **raw materials**, **work in progress** (WIP) and **finished goods**.

We must not forget that the auditor reviews not only the **amounts** included in the financial statements but also the way they are **presented** and **disclosed** – **classification** is the appropriate assertion here and the auditor will make sure that the relevant disclosure requirements are followed. Typically, disclosure includes:

> - **Accounting policies** used in calculating things such as cost and NRV are fully disclosed
>
> - Ensuring that inventory is **sub-classified** as **raw materials, WIP**, and **finished goods**
>
> (IAS 2: para.9)

Raw materials

Raw materials are tested to ensure that they are held at cost. This is because it is extremely unlikely that NRV would differ from cost for raw materials, unless they had been damaged or the value was affected by age.

First, auditors must understand how the company determines the cost of raw materials.

The company might be able to identify each item separately, in which case they can be valued at their own original cost.

However, it will not be possible to value some inventory in this way because of the nature of it, and the company will have to use a technique, such as first in first out (FIFO) which you should be aware of.

Work in progress (WIP)

You should know that accounting standards define 'cost' as 'cost of purchase plus the cost of conversion'.

The cost of conversion becomes relevant when considering WIP and finished goods. It will include:

- Directly attributable costs (for example, labour, machine costs)
- Other production costs (for example, lighting in the factory)

The auditors will need to test the company's calculation of cost of conversion. In general terms, the auditors may apply analytical procedures (for example, comparing similar inventory lines from this year to last year to see if any changes in price appear reasonable).

The allocation of production overheads must be done on the basis of normal activity, and the auditors must ensure that the overall calculations are reasonable.

Finished goods

Finished goods are most likely to be affected by NRV, as there is a market for them. WIP might also be affected by NRV, but this would be more difficult to judge.

NRV is the estimated or actual selling price of the goods.

The auditors should ensure any goods they noted as being obsolete or damaged at the inventory count have been reduced in value.

Activity 8: Hodgson Ltd

The following are extracts from the books and records of Hodgson Ltd, a manufacturer of garden equipment.

Required

Identify the audit work to be performed on these inventory balances, both individually and in aggregate.

	£
Raw materials	164,810
Work in progress	55,000
Finished goods	117,000
	336,810

Cut-off

Given the **sensitivity** of **statement of profit or loss items** like 'profit' and 'cost of sales' to recorded amounts of inventory, the main aim of the auditor is to ensure that there is **consistency** over **when** an amount of inventory is either purchased or sold. The aim is to apply the **matching concept**, especially at the very start and end of the reporting period to ensure inclusion in the correct year:

The **rule** is that income and expense is recorded at the point where the **risks** and **rewards** of ownership of that item are **transferred** (ie based on movement of inventory). The diagram below shows the treatment of items **in the financial statements for the year end** for items **sold** and **purchased** both **before** the year end and afterwards.

Illustration 2: Inventory cut-off

	Before	Year end	After

Revenues

Goods Despatched Note (GDN)

Included in:

– **Revenue** ✓
– Receivables ✓
– Inventory ✗

Purchases

Goods Received Note (GRN)

Included in:

– **Purchases** ✓
– Payables ✓
– Inventory ✓

Goods Despatched Note (GDN)

Included in:

– **Revenue** ✗
– Receivables ✗
– Inventory ✓

Goods Received Note (GRN)

Included in:

– **Purchases** ✗
– Payables ✗
– Inventory ✗

Cut-off tests for revenue

(1) Obtain last GDN number at year end

(2) Select a sample of GDNs raised before and after the year end, and ensure the revenue is accounted for in the correct period. Select a sample of sales invoices posted before and after the year end and ensure that GDNs are raised in the same period

Cut-off tests for purchases

As for revenues, but replace GDN with GRN and Sales Invoice with Purchase Invoice.

Activity 9: Cut-off testing

It is now the final audit of Glad Rags. The inventory cut-off information obtained by your audit firm at the inventory count is given below. The audit junior has obtained follow-up information to establish whether cut-off is correct, but is unsure what conclusion he should draw.

Required

Advise the junior whether he should refer the results of his revenue and purchases cut-off tests to his supervisor or not by highlighting the appropriate action. Materiality has been set at £50,000.

Client:	Glad Rags Ltd	Prepared by/Date:	A Junior 2/1/X5
Reporting date:	30 November 20X4	Reviewed by/Date:	

Inventory cut-off

Last deliveries out of the warehouse on 30/11/X4:

Sales order/GDN	Customer	Agreed to November Sales Day Book
200894/GDN 12403	J Club Ltd	✓
200895/GDN 12404	IZK Ltd	✓
200896/GDN 12405	Ginger Ltd	✓

The above revenue items have all been excluded from the inventory count and a receivable exists. I reviewed GDN 12406 to 12415 inclusive and all were included in the December Sales Day Book.

Last deliveries into the warehouse on 30/11/X4:

Purchase order/GRN	Supplier	Agreed to November Purchases Day Book
100552/GRN 1013	Fine Fabrics Ltd	✓
100553/GRN 1014	Fine Fabrics Ltd	✓
100554/GRN 1015	Terry's Threads	x

All the above purchase items were included in the inventory count but payables for Fine Fabrics only have been created at the year end. GRNs 1016 to 1025 inclusive were all included in the December Purchases Day Book.

The invoice for order 100554 was not received until 15 December and was included in December's Purchases Day Book. The value was £52,476. Terry's Threads has been included in the new year payables balance – the senior accountant explained that this was a regular order that arrived early.

Revenues cut-off testing: **No further action/Refer to supervisor**

Purchases cut-off testing: **No further action/Refer to supervisor**

2.3 Trade receivables

Trade receivables are the amount owed by customers in respect of credit sales.

Circularisation is a specific technique used to test the receivables balance by writing directly to customers owing money to the audited entity and asking them to confirm what they believe they owe. This can then be used to compare against the records held by the entity of sums owed by that customer and any discrepancies reconciled.

> **Illustration 3: Circularisation is conducted as follows:**
>
> (a) Obtain a **listing** of trade receivables, as at the year end.
>
> (b) **Agree the total** to sales ledger control account in the nominal ledger.
>
> (c) **Review** the listing for any obvious **omissions** or **misstatements**.
>
> (d) Select a **sample** of receivables accounts for **positive confirmation**. The letter should be on the **client's headed notepaper**, signed by the client with a copy of the current statement attached. It should request that the **reply** is **sent directly to the auditor** and reply-paid envelopes should be included.
>
> (e) After a **reasonable period**, the auditor should send **follow-up** requests by post.
>
> (f) If responses are still not forthcoming, then these should be followed up by **emails, phone calls** and **faxes**.
>
> (g) The auditor should **investigate** any **disputed balances**.
>
> (h) Often a **50% response rate** is the best that the auditor can ever hope for, but all **reasonable efforts** should be made to agree those receivables sampled where no reply is forthcoming. This is achieved by confirmation of individual outstanding invoices or alternative procedures such as verifying outstanding items to back up documentation, reviewing any cash received from that customer after the year end and discussions with the entity's credit controller.
>
> It is worth noting that circularisation is usually only a good test of **existence** and **rights and obligations**. It does not test valuations, as most customers will not confirm if the balance is understated, and agreeing that a debt is owed does not provide evidence that the debt will be settled.

A specimen receivables circularisation letter is given below:

WOODRIGHT LTD
24/26 Arthur Road
Newcastle upon Tyne
NT1 4LJ

Account: *107507*

To: *Rossney & Co.*
327 Skelworth Road
Aberdeen
AB11 4PR

5 January 20X8
Our ref: TCO/PJM/AUD

Dear Sir(s)

The balance on your account in our books at 31 December 20X7 is £*74,329.28* due from you.

We would be grateful if, for audit purposes, you could confirm your agreement of this balance by completing, signing and returning this form in the enclosed pre-paid envelope direct to our auditors, Tish & Co., Arlott House, 1 Wicket Lane, London NW1 3RT.

Remittances in settlement of amounts due should not be sent to our auditors.

If you cannot agree the balance, will you please note on the form the amount outstanding according to your records, together with such details you can provide of the differences. We shall be grateful for your co-operation in this matter.

Yours faithfully

PJ Marsh

The balance at *31/12/X7* (date) stated above is:

Agreed

Not agreed and the position according to our records is set out here

Please tick one box ☑

Invoice not yet received for- £12,454.33
∴ Balance agreed = £61,874.95

Signed *PE Carr*

Date *3/2/X8*

On behalf of *Rossney & Co.*

Activity 10: Circularisation

You are continuing your work at Glad Rags Ltd. The receivables circularised at the year end are listed below, along with information on the responses you have received and supporting information from Glad Rags. The reporting date is 30 November 20X4.

Required

Using all of the information given below, decide which of these balances requires referral to your supervisor.

Sample selected from sales ledger

	Amount owed per sales ledger	Response from customer	Other information supplied by customer
British Clothes Stores plc	484,536	439,598	Cheque in post
IZK Ltd	74,973	74,973	n/a
Tisco Stores plc	78,805	71,663	Disputed invoice
J Club Ltd	323,024	323,024	n/a
Cavanaghs Ltd	14,388	nil	Goods not received yet
H and T Ltd	18,933	nil	Cheques in post
Nice Clothes Ltd	17,231	nil	Cheques in post
Ginger Ltd	22,315	22,315	n/a

Cash book extracts (receipts)

Date	Details	Amount £
1 December 20X4	BCS sales ledger	44,938
10 December 20X4	H and T sales ledger	8,934
14 December 20X4	Nice Clothes sales ledger	7,392
12 January 20X4	H and T sales ledger	9,999
18 January 20X4	Nice Clothes sales ledger	9,839

Glad Rags warehouse despatch information

GDN 12398	28/11/20X4	British Clothes Stores plc	£23,399
GDN 12399	28/11/20X4	Value Mart plc	£12,778
GDN 12400	29/11/20X4	Cavanaghs Ltd	£14,388
GDN 12401	29/11/20X4	Tisco Stores plc	£78,805

Illustration 4: Other standard audit tests for receivables

	Audit objective		Example tests
(a)	Completeness/existence	(i)	Obtain **listing** of trade receivables and **reconcile** to nominal ledger.
		(ii)	Check details of **despatches** of goods around the year end and ensure they are correctly treated (ie recorded in the correct period for cut-off).
		(iii)	Check that a **sales invoice** has been raised for all despatches during the year.
		(iv)	Review after date **credit notes** issued.
(b)	Rights and obligations	(i)	Trace a sample of trade receivables to **cash received post year end**.
		(ii)	**Discuss** with management and/or review **board minutes** to establish whether any trade receivables have been **factored**.
(c)	Valuation	(i)	Review **consistency** of **policy** and its appropriateness.
		(ii)	Discuss significant **overdue debts** with a company official using a trade receivables **aged analysis**.
		(iii)	Review relevant **correspondence**.
		(iv)	Ensure all debts **written off** were properly authorised.
		(v)	Review allocation of after-date cash received.
(d)	Disclosure	(i)	Ensure trade receivables are appropriately **categorised** within current assets.
		(ii)	Ensure **classification** is correct as per Companies Act 2006 (trade receivables, other receivables, prepayments).

Activity 11: Pond Ltd

You are the audit senior on the audit of Pond Ltd, a gemstone dealer.

Required

Assuming that the largest balances will be selected, identify four other items from the sales ledger listing below that you would review, giving reasons for your selection.

Sales ledger listing

	£
Affectionado Ltd	76,002
Astra Stones Ltd	Nil
B. Trow Ltd	34,726
Bea Myan Ltd	7,013
Crystal Eyes plc	12,997
Engagement Centre Ltd	16,821
Gemba-Gems Ltd	22,032
Gemeyma Ltd	17,152
Jewels 'r' Us Ltd (> 90 days overdue)	3,294
Love Me Tender Ltd	6,111
Magnifique Ltd (> 60 days overdue)	987
Moonglow Ltd	1,342
Pearly Kween Ltd	812
Ruby-Dubie Ltd	467
Ring-ring Ltd	12,142
Wed-Me Ltd	(8,429)
	203,469

(1)

(2)

(3)

(4)

2.4 Cash and bank

Cash and bank will include all bank accounts held by the entity as well as any cash amounts held on site (such as petty cash and till floats).

The key audit test performed in the area of cash and bank is a review of the audited entity's **bank reconciliation** – a process designed to understand the timing differences between the entity's cash book and the bank's understanding of the entity's bank balance.

Activity 12: Bank reconciliation

You are the audit junior and have been given the bank reconciliation for the year ended 31 December 20X6 for Glad Rags.

Required

(a) **Identify and describe the audit tests that you should perform on the bank reconciliation.**

(b) **Select any item(s) that you would refer to the audit supervisor from your review.**

Bank reconciliation for Glad Rags as at 31 December 20X6

			£
Balance per bank statement			52,296.62
		£	£
Balance per statement			54,501.00
Less unpresented cheques			
	Cheque number:		
	010	7,834.53	
	695	19,721.87	
	696	17.98	
			(27,574.38)
Add outstanding lodgements			
	Lodgement number:		
	095	15,000.00	
	097	10,000.00	
			25,000.00
Add bank error			1,000.00
			52,926.62

(a) Audit tests to be performed on the bank reconciliation:

(b) Items to be referred to the audit supervisor (*select those that are appropriate*):

- Bank error
- Items to be written off
- Arithmetic
- Disclosure items
- Errors with source data

Illustration 5: Tests for cash and bank

Other than reviewing the bank reconciliation, other tests for cash and bank include:

	Audit objective		Example tests
(a)	Completeness/existence	(i)	Obtain **listing** of bank and cash balances and **reconcile** to nominal ledger.
		(ii)	Review bank confirmation letter for details of all accounts held.
		(iii)	Count petty cash balance.
		(iv)	Review cashbook for unusual items.
(b)	Rights and obligations	(i)	Review bank letter to ensure valid title to accounts held.
(c)	Disclosure	(i)	Review bank letter for any legal right to set off.
		(ii)	Investigate whether any accounts are secured over assets of the company.

Practice note 16 – bank report for audit purposes

The practice of obtaining **certificates** or **reports** from banks is an important feature in the proper discharge of the auditors' responsibilities. The **difficulty** for the auditor is getting hold of information regarding their client from a **third party** with whom they have **no direct contractual relationship**. The practice note sets out how both sides should act in this regard.

Procedures

- A standard letter should be sent in duplicate on each occasion by the auditor on his own note paper to each bank branch that the client holds an account at, or has had dealings with, since the end of the previous accounting period.

- Auditors should ensure that the bank receives their client's authority to permit disclosure of such information to a third party.

Contents of the letter

The **core information** requested in the standard letter is as follows:

(1)   Bank accounts and balances:

- Including details of any **restrictions** on accounts for balances
- Including details of **accounts closed** during the period

(2)   Details of **set-off arrangements**.

(3)   **Loans, overdrafts** and **associated covenants, guarantees** and **indemnities**, including term and repayment frequency

(4)   **Securities** charged with reference to items in (3) above

(5)   **Other banks** or **branches** where the customer has established a relationship during the period

The **supplementary information** requested in the **bank letter** is as follows:

(i)   Trade finance:

- **Bills** discounted with recourse
- Any **guarantees, bonds** or **indemnities** given to the bank by the customer on behalf of **third parties**
- Other **contingent liabilities**.

(ii)   Securities (Practice Note 16, Appendix 1).

2.5 Borrowings

Non-current liabilities are loans repayable at a date more than one year after the year end. Examples include bank loans and debentures (generally known as borrowings).

Auditors are concerned with completeness, valuation and disclosure.

Completeness

- Obtain/prepare a schedule of loans outstanding at the end of the reporting period.

- Compare opening balances to the previous year's working papers (closing balances at the end of last year).

- Test the clerical accuracy of the schedule.

- Compare balances to the general ledger.

- Check the names of lenders to relevant information (such as bank letter or register of debenture-holders).

- Review minutes and cash book to ensure that all loans have been recorded.

Valuation

- Trace additions and repayments to entries in the cash book.

- Confirm repayments are in accordance with the loan agreement.

- Examine receipts for loan repayments.

- Obtain direct confirmation from lenders about amounts loaned and the terms thereof.

- Verify interest charged for the period and the adequacy of accrued interest.

Disclosure

Review the disclosures made in the financial statements and ensure they meet legal requirements.

Activity 13: HEC Ltd

You have noted on the bank letter that your client, HEC Ltd, has a mortgage which is repayable over 20 years.

Required

Set out, in a format suitable for inclusion in an audit plan, the audit procedures to be carried out on this loan.

2.6 Payables

Payables are amounts the company owes to its suppliers.

Trade and other payables are not the largest credit balances on the statement of financial position (loans are usually far bigger) but there are various tests that need to be performed on them.

Activity 14: Gavilar Ltd

Required

Set out, in a manner suitable for inclusion in the audit plan, the audit procedures to be undertaken for each assertion in order to ensure that both trade and other payables are fairly stated in the financial statements of Gavilar Ltd.

Gavilar Ltd as at 31 December 20X7 Statement of financial position (extract)	
	£
Trade payables	476,870
Other payables	123,600
	600,470

Audit objective	Suggested audit procedures
Completeness	
Rights and obligations	
Valuation	
Existence	
Disclosure	

2.7 Provisions (accounting estimates)

An **accounting estimate** is an approximation of the amount of an item in the absence of a precise means of measurement. Examples include:

- Allowances to reduce inventories and receivables to their estimated realisable value
- Depreciation charges
- Accrued revenue
- Provision for a loss from a lawsuit
- Provision to meet warranty claims

A provision should be recognised when (i) a company has a **present obligation** (legal or constructive) where (ii) a **probable** outflow of resources embodying economic benefits will be necessary to settle it and (iii) that benefit can be **reliably estimated** (IAS 37: para. 14).

Directors and management are responsible for making accounting estimates included in the financial statements. These estimates are often made in conditions of **uncertainty** regarding the outcome of events and involve the use of judgement. The risk of a material misstatement therefore increases when accounting estimates are involved (and thus inherent risk is higher). **Audit evidence** supporting accounting estimates is generally less than conclusive and so auditors need to exercise **significant judgement**.

Accounting estimates may be produced as part of the routine operations of the accounting system, or may be a non-routine procedure at the period end. Where, as is frequently the case, a **formula** based on past experience is used to calculate the estimate, it should be reviewed regularly by management (for example, actual vs estimate in prior periods).

Audit procedures

The auditors should gain an understanding of the procedures and methods used by management to make accounting estimates. This will aid the auditors' planning of their own procedures. Auditors must carry out one or a mixture of the following procedures.

Procedure 1 – Review and testing the process

The auditors should:

- Evaluate the data and consider the assumptions on which the estimate is based
- Test the calculations involved in the estimate
- Compare estimates made for prior periods with actual results of those periods
- Consider management's/directors' review and approval procedures

Procedure 2 – Use of an independent estimate

Such an estimate (made or obtained by the auditors) may be compared with the accounting estimate.

Procedure 3 – Review of subsequent events

The auditors should review transactions or events after the period end which may reduce or even remove the need to test accounting estimates. For example, if directors have estimated an allowance for an irrecoverable debt, but all debt existing at the end of the reporting period has been paid by the date of the auditor's report, this provision will no longer be required (ISA 540: para. 13).

2.8 Revenue

Revenue is often tested at the same time as **receivables**, due to it being the other side of the double entry. Revenue testing is usually done by **analytical procedures**: it should be possible to see **predictable relationships** arising.

Key assertions relating to revenue are completeness and accuracy. The auditor wants to confirm that all relevant revenue has been included and that revenue actually does relate to the correct year.

Completeness

Revenue is often tested by analytical procedures, as there is usually a great deal of information available in a company about its revenue and it should be possible to see predictable relationships arising.

Auditors should:

- Review the level of revenue over the year, comparing it on a month by month basis with previous years

- Consider the effect that any price rises have had on both the quantity of items sold and the amount of revenue received

- Consider the level of goods returned, sales allowances and discounts.

In addition, the auditors may test the completeness of recording of revenue in the original records, for example, tracing from documents that first record revenue right through to the general ledger.

So, for example, the auditor may trace through from a sales order to a goods despatch note to a sales invoice to the sales day book to the sales ledger to the general ledger.

In a cash business, the auditor may trace from the till roll to the sales day book to the sales ledger to the general ledger.

Accuracy

The auditors should also check that revenue has been measured correctly by:

- Checking calculations and additions on sales invoices
- Ensuring VAT has been dealt with appropriately
- Checking discounts have been applied properly
- Checking the casting of the sales ledger accounts and control account

2.9 Payroll

When the auditors are scrutinising payroll-related payables, they may also carry out substantive procedures on payroll expense, which is highly likely to be material to the financial statements.

A great deal of testing may be done by analytical procedures, as there are a number of predictable relationships (number of staff, standard rates of pay, ratio of deductions to pay etc).

However, the auditor may also carry out tests of detail in relation to occurrence, measurement and completeness.

Occurrence

- Check individual remuneration per payroll to personnel records.
- Confirm existence of employees by meeting them.
- Check benefits to supporting documentation.

Accuracy

- Recalculate benefits.
- Check whether deductions of tax and NI have been made correctly.
- Check validity of other deductions, eg pension contributions to conditions of pension scheme.

Completeness

- Check a sample of employees from records to the payroll.
- Check whether joiners have been paid in the correct month.
- Check whether leavers have been correctly removed from payroll.
- Check casts of the payroll.
- Confirm payment of pay to bank transfer records.
- Agree net pay per cash book to payroll.
- Scrutinise payroll and investigate unusual items.

2.10 Other expenses – Purchases

When testing purchases, auditors are concerned with whether they have occurred, whether they are measured correctly, and whether they have been made for valid business reasons.

We have already considered the issue of cut-off on purchases in relation to inventory.

Occurrence

The auditors often test purchases by using analytical procedures.

Auditors should:

- Consider the level of purchases on a month by month basis compared with previous years
- Consider the effect on value of purchases of price changes
- Consider the effect on value of purchases of changes in products purchased
- Compare the ratio of trade payables to purchases with previous years
- Compare the ratio of trade payables to inventory with previous years
- Consider the level of major expenses other than purchases in comparison with previous years

In addition, the auditors may test the completeness of recording of purchases in the original records − for example, tracing documents that first record purchases right through to the general ledger.

Also, to check the validity of purchases in the records, the auditors may test individual items in the nominal ledger back through the records to the original purchase order and requisition.

Activity 15: Adjustments

Required

Indicate whether the following matters require to be adjusted or not.

The auditor has found an invoice for office supplies ordered and delivered on the last day of the financial year. The invoice amount has not been included in the total for purchases in the statement of profit or loss. The amount for these supplies is material.	▼
The auditor has completed analytical review of the cost of sales for a bakery. This analysis has indicated that ingredient costs per loaf have increased from 12.8 pence in the previous year to a figure closer to £3.56 per loaf. The non-financial information on numbers of loaves has been corroborated during the audit.	▼
The auditor has selected 20 payments from the purchase ledger total and has been tracing them back to invoices for evidence of both existence and valuation. Of these 20 payments, 19 have been traced successfully back for both assertions. The 20th item has no invoice and relates to health and safety assessments carried out at the entity's head office. A similar amount was included in last year's statement of profit or loss and this year's figure can be agreed back to a quotation that the chief accountant was sent by the contractor. The audit senior has recorded evidence of this assessment within the current file as part of the firm's wider audit testing.	▼

Picklist:

Requires to be adjusted
Does not require to be adjusted

2.11 Other payables (accruals)

Other payables or accruals are made when an entity **receives** a **product or service** for which it has **not yet paid (such as a utilities bill)**. To **test** other payables, the auditors will:

- Verify the valuation, existence and completeness of such items by reference to **subsequent payments**

- Verify the calculation of the item for **reasonableness** in light of all supporting evidence (for example, review statement of profit and loss and prior years to consider whether other accruals are required)

- Perform **analytical procedures** to assess if additional payables are required

- Review payments made and invoices received **after the year end** to ascertain if they should have been accrued

PAYE and VAT accruals can be verified by reference to the monthly payroll deductions and the next VAT return.

2.12 Other receivables (prepayments)

Other receivables or prepayments occur when a company pays for an expense **in advance of receiving the item** – examples of this could include **insurance** premiums, **rental** of **property** or even a **telephone line**. To **test** other receivables, auditors will:

- Trace the relevant payments to both **cash book** and **invoice** to test **existence**

- **Review** the calculation of the payment for **accuracy**

- Review the statement of profit and loss to ensure that all likely prepayments have been accounted for

- Perform **analytical procedures** to assess whether they seem **reasonable**

Activity 16: Miscellaneous procedures

Required

For each of the following listed procedures, identify the most appropriate area of the financial statements that is being tested from the picklist below.

Consider the effect of any price rises during the year.		▼
Review sales ledger for old receivables which are still unpaid.		▼
Verify amount outstanding by reference to subsequent payments.		▼
Perform analytical procedures by comparing payments with previous years to see if they appear reasonable.		▼
Recalculate amounts due in relation to tax and national insurance payable by employees.		▼

Picklist:

A prepaid insurance premium
An allowance for a doubtful debt
An accrual for an unpaid electricity bill
Cash sales from a retail outlet
Deductions paid to HM Revenue & Customs (HMRC)

- Auditors need to be able to explain the areas of audit risk that lead to material misstatements in the financial statements – this is likely to be tested as a written exercise in your assessment.

- Audit procedures exist for a variety of assertions depending on the area of the financial statements under review and again you will need to be able to produce written procedures as part of your assessment:

  - Non-current assets – capitalisation and relevant assertions

  - Inventory – the role of the inventory count, plus specific tests for different types of inventory (raw materials, work in progress or WIP and finished goods) and how to test for the correct treatment around the year end (cut-off)

  - Receivables – procedures are focused on circularisation (including the process itself and analysing the outcome of such a process)

  - Cash and bank – two key controls exist in this area (the bank letter and the bank reconciliation) so you need to be able to explain how each works

  - Borrowings – loans and other long-term liabilities

  - Payables – trade and others

  - Allowances – including depreciation, impairments to inventory and write-downs on doubtful debts

  - Revenue – using double entry to prove this amount by comparison with receivables

  - Payroll – again, using double entry to verify this amount as an expense in the statement of profit or loss

  - Purchases – includes any other expenses

  - Accruals – amounts due that have not yet been paid for but require recognising in the financial statements

  - Prepayments – amounts not yet due but paid which also require reconciliation to ensure they are not misstated

Keywords

- **Accounting estimate:** an approximation of the amount of an item in the absence of a precise means of measurement

- **Bank reconciliation:** a process designed to understand the timing differences between the entity's cash book and the bank's understanding of the entity's bank balance

- **Cash and bank:** will include all bank accounts held by the entity as well as any cash amounts held on site (such as petty cash and till floats)

- **Circularisation:** a specific technique used to test the receivables balance by writing directly to customers owing money to the audited entity and asking them to confirm what they believe they owe

- **Finance lease:** a lease that transfers substantially all the risks and rewards of ownership of an asset to the lessee. Title may or may not be eventually transferred

- **Inventory:** sub-classified as raw materials, work in progress (WIP), and finished goods

- **Lease:** a contract between a lessor and a lessee for the hire of a specific asset

- **Non-current assets:** assets held for continuing use in the business

- **Non-current liabilities:** loans repayable at a date more than one year after the year end. Examples include bank loans and debentures (generally known as borrowings)

- **Operating lease:** a lease other than a finance lease

- **Other payables or accruals:** made when an entity receives a product or service for which it has not yet paid (such as a utilities bill)

- **Other receivables or prepayments:** occur when a company pays for an expense in advance of receiving the item – examples of this could include insurance premiums, rental of property or even a telephone line

- **Payables:** amounts the company owes to its suppliers

- **Trade receivables:** the amount owed by customers in respect of credit sales

1   Select whether the following statements are true or false.

Inventory is difficult to audit because it often consists of a large number of low value items which are collectively material.	▼
Key assertions to test in relation to inventory are existence, completeness and valuation.	▼

Picklist:

True
False

2   Select whether the following statements are true or false.

It is important to record cut-off correctly so that assets are not double counted (receivables and inventory).	▼
It is important to record cut-off correctly so that a liability is not omitted in respect of an asset (payables and inventory).	▼
For the purposes of the financial statements, it does not matter if the company misstates cut-off between raw materials and work in progress.	▼

Picklist:

True
False

3   The objective of a substantive procedure will determine the source of evidence obtained.

For each of the objectives set out below, select the source of evidence.

Obtain evidence of the value of raw material	▼
Obtain evidence of the value of finished goods	▼

Picklist:

Both
Purchase invoice
Sales invoice

4 Complete the following statements about how net realisable value is tested.

Net realisable value is tested with reference to after the year end [▼].

The value of items of inventory is compared to post year end [▼].

This is to ensure that inventory value is equal to or [▼] than net realisable value of the inventory.

Picklist for line items:

Higher
Lower
Purchases
Purchase invoices
Sales
Sales invoices

5 Auditors will carry out the following tests when auditing inventory.

From the options provided, select which important assertion about inventory each test is seeking to prove in the first instance.

Attending an inventory count	▼
Tracing counted items to final inventory sheets	▼
Reviewing after year end sales invoices	▼

Picklist:

Completeness
Existence
Valuation

6 Select which of the following statements best summarises the assertions the auditors are concerned with in respect of non-current assets by ticking the appropriate box.

Auditors are concerned with completeness, existence, rights and obligations and valuation. ☐

Auditors are concerned with completeness, existence and valuation. ☐

Auditors are concerned with existence, valuation and occurrence. ☐

Auditors are concerned with existence, valuation, occurrence and accuracy. ☐

7   Auditors usually test receivables by carrying out a circularisation and/or review of receipts after the year end.

Select which assertions the auditors are seeking evidence about.

Receivables circularisation	▼
Reviewing sales and receipts after year end	▼

Picklist:

Both
Rights and obligations
Valuation

8   Select which of the following statements concerning the audit of revenue is incorrect by ticking the appropriate box.

Auditors usually rely 100% on controls over revenue by carrying out only controls testing.   ☐

Auditors may test controls over revenue but will also carry out some substantive procedures, often restricted to analytical procedures as there is usually ample evidence concerning a company's revenue.   ☐

Auditors will often only test revenue by analytical procedures as there is usually ample evidence concerning a company's revenue.   ☐

Auditors will sometimes test completeness of revenue by tracing a sample of revenue from sales order to general ledger.   ☐

9   State whether the following statements are true or false in respect of bank letter requests.

Bank letter requests are sent out by the auditor directly to the bank.	▼
Bank letter requests should be made at the year end date.	▼
Auditors will commonly test cash balances even if they are not material.	▼

Picklist:

True
False

10 Select which of the following statements best summarises the issues that auditors are concerned with in respect of trade payables by ticking the appropriate box.

Auditors are concerned with completeness, existence and valuation. ☐

Auditors are concerned with completeness, existence and obligations. ☐

Auditors are concerned with existence, obligations and occurrence. ☐

Auditors are concerned with existence, obligations, occurrence and accuracy. ☐

11 State whether the following statements are true or false in respect of supplier statements.

They represent a better source of evidence than replies to a receivables circularisation as they are sent direct to the company.	▼
They are only used when the auditor is unable to do a payables circularisation.	▼
Testing supplier statements provides evidence that trade payables have not been understated.	▼

Picklist:

True
False

12 Complete the following statements about selecting a sample of trade payables.

Auditors should consider that payables might be [▼] and therefore not simply select large balances to test (although they must select [▼] items).

[▼] balances should also be incorporated into the test.

Picklist for line items:

Material
Nil
Overstated
Significant
Understated

13 Complete the following definitions.

[_____ ▼] are liabilities other than [_____ ▼] that arise because the company has received a benefit it has not yet paid for.

[_____ ▼] are loans repayable at a date [_____ ▼] one year after the year end.

Picklist for line items:

Accruals
Equal to
Less than
More than
Non-current liabilities
Other payables
Trade payables

14 Select which of the following statements best summarises the issues that auditors are concerned with in respect of payroll expense by ticking the appropriate box.

Auditors are concerned with completeness, existence and valuation. ☐

Auditors are concerned with completeness, existence and obligations. ☐

Auditors are concerned with occurrence, accuracy and completeness. ☐

Auditors are concerned with existence, obligations, occurrence and accuracy. ☐

15 Set out the types of accruals you would expect to exist at a manufacturer and the audit procedures that should be carried out on each.

Evaluation

6

Learning outcomes

6.1	**Examine the role of audit working papers**
	• The role of audit documentation in providing evidence as a basis for the auditor's opinion
	• The importance of retaining working papers for future reference
	• Form and content of working papers
6.2	**Select and justify matters to be referred to a senior colleague**
	• Identify material and immaterial misstatements
	• Identify deviations from an audited entity's prescribed procedures
	• Identify matters of unusual nature and unauthorised transactions, unusual events.
	– Non-routine transactions
	– Related party transactions
	– Transactions above or below market rates
	– Suspected fraud
6.3	**Evaluate audit evidence and recommend a suitable audit opinion**
	• Identify a suitable audit opinion arising from
	• Significant uncertainties
	• Material misstatements
	• Inability to obtain sufficient, appropriate evidence (limitation on scope)
6.4	**Effectively report audit findings to management**
	• Identify the consequences of deficiencies in internal controls how the deficiencies can be remedied

Assessment context

This topic covers four tasks in the assessment, one of which (identifying the consequences of deficiencies in internal control) is a written assessment so you should consider how to respond accordingly using the suggested activity.

Qualification context

As this is the final topic of this unit, there is an element of bringing the syllabus together so there will be plenty that you have seen before here. In order to report on the truth and fairness of the financial statements, you also need to know what they include, so expect to see some financial reporting elements within tasks set.

Business context

For many audit firms, evaluation is the most important element of the whole audit, where any outstanding issues are addressed prior to communicating the all-important opinion. For others, the audit opinion is merely the formality attached to the end of a process, necessary only to fulfil a legal obligation.

The audit profession in the 21st century is under enormous pressure to consider its future in the wake of ongoing financial reporting scandals: some outside observers feel that auditors should be subject to greater competition and regulation and be more responsible for the mistakes made by their clients, while others feel that putting too much pressure on the auditor will simply force many of them out of this line of work, leaving a skills and experience vacuum that could impact on quality and therefore increase the risk of mistakes being made by entities. The debate rages on!

Chapter overview

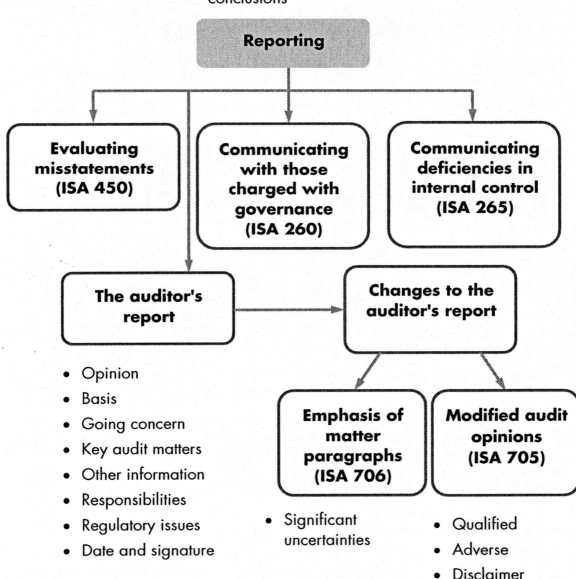

Documentation (working papers)

- Audit procedures
- Regulatory and legal compliance
- Best practice
- Judgement and conclusions

Reporting

Evaluating misstatements (ISA 450)

Communicating with those charged with governance (ISA 260)

Communicating deficiencies in internal control (ISA 265)

The auditor's report

- Opinion
- Basis
- Going concern
- Key audit matters
- Other information
- Responsibilities
- Regulatory issues
- Date and signature

Changes to the auditor's report

Emphasis of matter paragraphs (ISA 706)

- Significant uncertainties

Modified audit opinions (ISA 705)

- Qualified
- Adverse
- Disclaimer

1 Audit documentation

In order to reach a conclusion, the auditor has to make sense of all the information obtained during the audit – some of which will be more material than others. There are protocols for storing and recording such evidence which are laid down in ISA 230 *Audit Documentation*. The ISA clarifies the role of documentation as:

- Evidence of the auditor's basis for a conclusion about the achievement of the overall objectives of the auditor (ultimately supporting the audit opinion)

- Evidence that the audit was planned and performed in accordance with ISAs and applicable legal and regulatory requirements

- Physical or electronic media (audit files) for storing working papers and other records specific to the audit engagement.

(ISA 230: paras. 2 and 6)

Often this documentation is referred to as **working papers**.

Working papers are the documentation prepared by and for, or obtained and retained by, the auditor in connection with the performance of the audit (ISA 230: para. 6).

Activity 1: Documentation

Required

What additional purposes do you think audit documentation might serve?

Auditors must reference working papers with a number of details:

- Name (or initials) of the auditor who prepared the working paper
- Date the working paper was prepared
- Area of the audit being worked on (for example, inventory)
- Identifying characteristics of the item/matters being tested
- Period end of the financial statements being audited

Working papers are reviewed by a member of staff more senior than the one that prepared them. When a working paper is reviewed, the reviewer also initials the working paper and dates when it was reviewed.

1.1 Document what?

ISA 230 sets out what auditors must document in a general rule:

'The auditor shall prepare audit documentation on a timely basis' (ISA 230: para. 7).

The auditor shall prepare audit documentation that is sufficient to enable an experienced auditor, having no previous connection with the audit, to understand:

- 'The **nature, timing and extent of the audit procedures** performed to comply with the ISAs and applicable legal and regulatory requirements;

- The **results** of the audit procedures performed, and the **audit evidence obtained**; and

- **Significant matters** arising during the audit, the **conclusions reached** thereon, and **significant professional judgements** made in reaching those conclusions.'

This includes information on:

- Planning the audit
- The nature, timing and extent of the audit procedures performed
- Results of the audit procedures and the audit evidence obtained
- Conclusions drawn from audit evidence obtained from procedures
- Any contentious issues and how they were resolved
- Discussions on significant matters had with client staff/officers

Auditors must document their reasoning on significant matters where they have exercised judgement and the conclusions they have drawn and how they addressed any inconsistencies between evidence originally collected and the auditor's final conclusions on any matters (so, if the auditor's view on internal controls changes through the course of the audit, there should be documentation to explain this change of viewpoint).

Here is an example of a working paper on payables from The Heavenly Eating Company (HEC) Ltd:

Client: _The HEC Ltd_

Subject: _Payables_

Year end: _31 December 20X7_

Prepared by	Reviewed by
_PC_	
Date: _16.2.X8_	Date:

_H³/₁_

Work done	Selected a sample of trade payables as at 31 December and reconciled the supplier's statement to the year end purchase ledger balance. Vouched any reconciling items to source documentation.

Results   See H°/₂

One credit note, relating to Ambrosia Ltd. has not been accounted for. An adjustment is required.

| DEBIT | Trade payables | £1,327 | |
| CREDIT | Purchases | | £1,327 H1/₂ |

One other error was found, which was immaterial, and which was the fault of the supplier.

In view of the error found, however, we should recommend that the client management checks supplier statement reconciliations at least on the larger accounts. Management letter point.

Conclusion

After making the adjustment noted above, purchased ledger balances are fairly stated as at 31 December 20X7

1.2 Document how much?

The ISA suggests that the auditor should write down enough that an experienced auditor who has no experience of the particular client could follow and understand what had been done (ISA 230: para. 8).

The form, content and extent of audit documentation will depend on factors such as:

- The nature of the audit procedures
- Risks of material misstatement
- The extent of judgement required
- The significance of the evidence
- The nature and extent of exceptions identified

In other words, the auditor will need to use his judgement in making this decision.

1.3 Standardisation of working papers

There may be cases where working papers, for example checklists or specimen letters, are standardised, so that the auditor merely has to complete the client details. However, the auditor must always take care when using standardised

working papers; as it is never appropriate to take a mechanical approach to auditing, audit judgement must always be exercised.

Audit files

Working papers usually include:

- Information about the entity and its environment
- Evidence of the audit planning process
- Evidence of the auditor's consideration of the internal audit function (if relevant)
- Analyses of transactions and balances in the financial statements
- Analyses of significant ratios and trends
- Identified and assessed risks of material misstatements
- Record of the nature, timing and extent of resulting procedures
- Copies of letters concerning matters communicated to, or discussed with, management such as the terms of the engagement
- Conclusions reached by the auditor on significant aspects of the audit
- Copies of the financial statements and auditor's report

For one audit, this can amount to a lot of working papers. Working papers are therefore contained in **audit files**.

> **Audit regulations usually require that working papers must be kept for at least six years from the end of the accounting period to which they relate.**

Activity 2: Working papers

Required

Identify the purposes of each of the working papers in the table below by selecting the most appropriate reason for their preparation.

Working paper	Reason for preparation
A register of shares in audit client companies owned by staff members	▽
A copy of an email sent by the finance director of Curtis Ltd explaining a bid that has been made to acquire the company	▽
Briefing notes for the audit team before the start of the audit of Gordon Ltd	▽
A reconciliation of circularised responses to a list of receivables for an audit client	▽

Picklist:

Demonstrating legal, regulatory and ethical compliance by the auditor
Planning, directing, supervision and review of the audit engagement
Recording matters from an audit that are either unusual or significant
Supporting audit evidence for the auditor's opinion

2 Reporting matters to appropriate individuals

Once all completion procedures have been satisfactorily addressed, the auditor should have all the evidence required to reach the necessary conclusions for the audit opinion. In order to completely discharge both legal and best practice responsibilities, the auditor now has a number of reporting tasks to complete:

- Ensuring that all material and significant errors, deficiencies or other variations from standard are reported internally within the firm (ISA 450)

- Ensuring that such findings are reported to those charged with governance within the entity (ISAs 260 and 265)

- Ensuring that the shareholders are given the most appropriate audit report that reflects the auditor's experience (ISAs 700, 705 and 706)

2.1 ISA 450 *Evaluation of Misstatements Identified During the Audit*

It is almost inevitable that, during the course of the audit, a number of **misstatements** will be **uncovered**, some of them **material**, others clearly **trivial**. The auditor needs guidance to ensure that all such misstatements are both identified and recorded and that the most appropriate action is taken as a result.

The auditor must maintain a record of **all identified misstatements** (except those that are clearly trivial). As part of completion procedures, the auditor must evaluate the effect of these identified misstatements on the audit and the effect of uncorrected misstatements on the financial statements.

ISA 450 *Evaluation of Misstatements Identified During the Audit* gives guidance about this. The auditor must consider if the audit strategy and plan need revision if:

- The nature and circumstances of identified misstatements indicate that other unidentified misstatements exist, the combined total of which might be material.

- The aggregate of identified misstatements approaches the materiality level set by the auditors during planning (ISA 450: para. 6).

The auditors must make management aware of identified misstatements and request that they are adjusted. If they refuse, the auditors should take their reasons into account when evaluating if the financial statements as a whole are free from material misstatement.

Before assessing the effect uncorrected misstatements have on the financial statements, the auditors should reconfirm that the materiality level remains appropriate. They should then determine whether the aggregate of the uncorrected misstatements is material.

The auditors should communicate the uncorrected misstatements to those charged with governance (listed individually). They should obtain a written representation from management and, where appropriate, from those charged with governance about whether they believe the uncorrected misstatements to be immaterial.

In addition to the list of uncorrected misstatements, the auditors should document the level below which items will be considered trivial and the auditor's conclusion as to whether uncorrected misstatements are material, and the reasons for that conclusion (ISA 450: paras. 7 to 15).

2.2 ISA 260 *Communication with Those Charged with Governance*

The auditor then completes this reporting task by **informing** those charged with governance at the entity (remember that these will be board members who have a **right** to such information as they act **on behalf of the shareholders**) of any **uncorrected misstatements** and their **impact on the financial statements**, requesting formal **acknowledgement** that they accept these

misstatements and believe them to be **immaterial** to the financial statements. They will also report any other issues that may have been discovered during the audit (such as the availability of information or any delays in providing necessary audit evidence).

Such an acknowledgement comes as part of **written representations** under ISA 580 *Written Representations* and is added to the auditor's documentation, which lists all such misstatements as one of the following:

- Clearly trivial, as they fall below a threshold specified by the auditor

- Those that have been identified and corrected during the course of the audit

- Uncorrected misstatements, along with the auditor's conclusion as to whether they are material or not (ISA 580: Appendix 2).

Activity 3: Glad Rags

The audit junior is reviewing his working papers for the audit of Glad Rags and has requested your help in dealing with two issues that were not previously reported.

Required

In respect of each of these matters, select whether the audit junior should take no further action or refer it to the supervisor.

When reviewing the bank statements, the chief accountant removed some of the pages relating to the period of time after the year end.	No further action Refer it to the supervisor
During his review of the payroll system, incorrect PAYE income tax rates were found to have been used. This was retrospectively corrected for the following month and all supporting transactions reviewed by the junior.	No further action Refer it to the supervisor

2.3 ISA 265 Communicating Deficiencies in Internal Control to those Charged with Governance and Management

A **deficiency in internal control** is when a control is designed, implemented or operated in such a way that it is unable to prevent, or detect and correct, misstatements in the financial statements on a timely basis, or a necessary control is missing (ISA 265: para. 6(a)).

'The auditor shall determine whether, on the basis of the audit work performed, the auditor has identified one or more **deficiencies in internal control**. If the auditor has identified one or more deficiencies in internal control, the auditor shall determine, on the basis of the audit work performed, whether, individually or in combination, they constitute **significant deficiencies**. The auditor shall **communicate in writing** significant deficiencies in internal control identified during the audit **to those charged with governance on a timely basis** (ISA 265, para.10).'

The auditor's **judgement** is called into question here to determine what merits 'significant' but we will look at this later. The process of communication to those charged with governance will include **non-executive directors** who represent shareholders.

The auditor shall also communicate to **management** at an appropriate level of responsibility on a **timely basis**:

(a) **In writing**, significant deficiencies in internal control that the auditor has communicated or intends to communicate to those charged with governance, **unless it would be inappropriate to communicate directly to management in the circumstances**

The auditor may suspect that members of management may be involved in **fraud** – reporting this would be technically in line with the ISA but might breach certain criminal protocols (such as '**tipping off**' when dealing with money laundering).

(b) **Other deficiencies** in internal control identified during the audit that have not been communicated to management by **other parties** and that, in the auditor's professional judgment, are of **sufficient importance to merit management's attention** (ISA 265, para.10).'

Other parties involved here might include internal auditors or regulators, allowing the external auditor to inform management of their findings.

'The auditor shall include in the written communication of **significant deficiencies** in internal control:

(a) A **description** of the deficiencies and an **explanation** of their potential effects

(b) Sufficient information to enable those charged with governance and management to understand the **context** of the communication. In particular, the auditor shall explain that:

   (i) The purpose of the audit was for the auditor to express an **opinion on the financial statements**

   (ii) The audit included consideration of internal control relevant to the preparation of the financial statements in order to design audit procedures that are appropriate in the circumstances, but **not for the purpose of expressing an opinion on the effectiveness of internal control**

   (iii) The matters being reported are **limited to those deficiencies that the auditor has identified during the audit** and that the auditor has concluded are of **sufficient importance** to merit being reported to those charged with governance.'

(ISA 265: para. 11)

Significant means 'in the auditor's opinion, matters that warrant the attention of those charged with governance.'

(ISA 265: para. 6(b))

Activity 4: Reporting recommendations

Accounting system information – Glad Rags Revenue system

The company manufactures clothes to order from a catalogue. When an order is received, the sales department checks that the customer has not exceeded their credit limit and then issues a two-part order document. The sales department fills in the appropriate values for the order from current price lists. One copy is sent to the production department in order for the order to be completed and the other is filed alphabetically in the customer file in the sales department.

Once the order is completed, two-part despatch notes are raised. When the factory manager, Ian Jones, has checked the order, one copy of the despatch note is despatched with the goods (to be signed and returned), and one part is matched to the production department's sales order and sent to accounts to raise the invoice. Jane Hill raises the invoices from the order and despatch note, enters them on the computer and sends them out to customers.

Most customers pay in around 60 days. When they come in, cheques are passed to Beth Simpkins, one of the accounts assistants, and she updates the cash book and the sales ledger. Cheques are banked twice a week. Cheques are kept securely in the safe until banking.

Jane sends out statements to customers each month. Glad Rags' customers are mostly all reputable high street stores and there are rarely irrecoverable debts.

Required

Set out two deficiencies in the accounting systems for revenues at Glad Rags Limited as described above to be included in a report to those charged with governance. You should also set out the possible consequence of each deficiency and your recommendation for improvement.

| **Deficiency** | **Deficiency** |

| **Consequence** | **Consequence** |

| **Recommendation** | **Recommendation** |

3 ISA 700 (revised) *Forming an Opinion and Reporting on Financial Statements*

You already know that the primary objective of the audit is an expression of an **opinion** on the **truth** and **fairness** (or **fair presentation**) of the **financial statements**. The format of the auditor's report is laid down in ISA 700 (revised):

INDEPENDENT AUDITOR'S REPORT

To the shareholders of the company [*or other appropriate addressee.*]

Opinion

[*Includes the individual statements and the reporting period under review for the company being audited. It can use either 'give a true and fair view' or 'presents fairly, in all material respects' and states the relevant GAAP adopted.*]

Basis for opinion

[*This is always presented after the opinion and explains how the audit was conducted: the role of ISAs and the IESBA code of ethics as well as the audit evidence being sufficient and appropriate to provide a basis for the auditor's opinion.*]

Material uncertainty relating to going concern

[*Where applicable, the auditor shall report in accordance with ISA 570 (Revised) Going Concern*]

Key audit matters

[*As per ISA 701 Key Audit Matters, matters of most significance from the audit; usually only required for listed entities.*]

Other information

[*As per ISA 720 Other Information, communicates that there is nothing to report regarding other information.*]

Responsibilities of management and those charged with governance for the financial statements

[*Preparation and fair presentation of the financial statements, including internal controls, and the assessment of the company's ability to continue as a going concern.*]

Auditor's responsibilities for the audit of the financial statements

[*A detailed summary of the auditor's objectives, starting with obtaining reasonable assurance about the financial statements being free from material misstatements due to fraud or error. Stresses the role of professional judgement and scepticism over accounting policies and estimates, judgements, internal controls, presentation, disclosure and communicating key audit matters and other issues with those charged with governance.*]

> **Report on other legal and regulatory requirements**
>
> *[Form and content of this section of the auditor's report will vary depending on the nature of the auditor's other reporting responsibilities.]*
>
> **Signed**
>
> *[Auditor's name and/or signature, address and date of the auditor's report.]*
>
> (ISA 700: Appendix)

Please note that ISA 701 is not currently examinable; it has been included here for the sake of completeness.

4 Changes to the auditor's report

In some cases, the standard report with unmodified opinion **may not be appropriate**. We shall now look at the **various circumstances** that lead to such variations in the auditor's report and what each one should take into account.

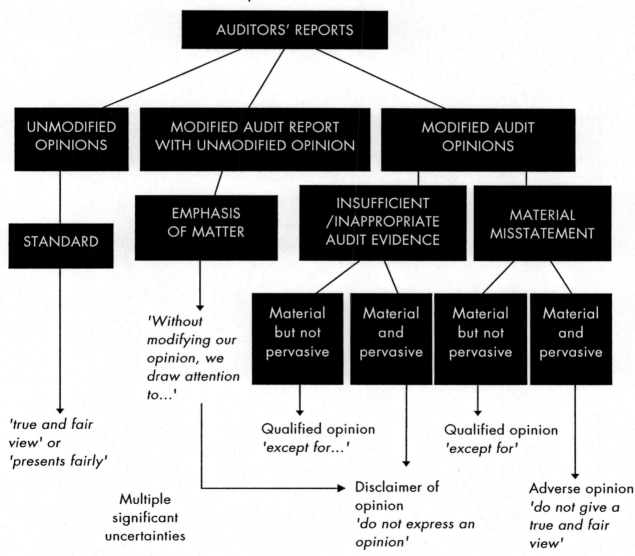

4.1 ISA 706 (revised) *Emphasis of Matter paragraphs and Other Matter Paragraphs in the Independent Auditor's Report*

In the auditor's opinion, it may be **necessary** to **draw users' attention** to matters appropriately presented and disclosed **within the financial statements** that are of such importance they are **fundamental** to users' understanding of either the financial statements themselves or the rest of the audit itself (including the auditor's responsibilities and their report).

An **emphasis of matter** paragraph draws users' attention to issues **within the financial statements** that they need to see in order to understand them properly, such as:

- Significant uncertainties relating to future outcomes of exceptional litigation or regulatory action

- A significant subsequent event that occurs between the date of the financial statements and the date of the auditor's report

- Early application of a new accounting standard that has a material effect on the financial statements

- A major catastrophe that has had, or continues to have, a significant effect on the entity's financial position

This emphasis of matter paragraph should be added **after the opinion paragraph**, using the heading **'Emphasis of Matter',** including **full details** of the matter and the **location** within the financial statements that explains the issue further.

The paragraph states that the auditor's opinion is **not modified in respect of this matter** – the use of such a paragraph **must only occur** if the matter in question has already been **adequately treated and disclosed** in the financial statements and the auditor is in agreement with this (ISA 706: paras. 6, A4, A5, A16 and Appendix 3).

Activity 5: Emphasis of matter paragraphs

Required

In respect of the matter described below, select the most appropriate course of action for the auditor to take.

You are the auditor for a supermarket. A customer has eaten own-brand produce and suffered an allergic reaction to one of the ingredients. The customer is currently claiming punitive damages for insufficient information on the food label. If successful, the damages would represent a material amount to the company. The company was successfully sued for a similar event three years ago, so has created a provision for this and has disclosed the matter in full in its financial statements.	Unmodified opinion with emphasis of matter paragraph Unmodified opinion with no further modification to the audit report

4.2 ISA 705 (revised) *Modifications to the Opinion in the Independent Auditor's Report*

There are **three types** of **modified opinion** that the auditor can issue (depending on the **nature of the matter** giving rise to the modification and the **pervasiveness** of that matter on the financial statements):

> (1) A qualified opinion
>
> (2) An adverse opinion
>
> (3) A disclaimer of opinion.

The types of modification can be summarised as follows by considering the **judgements** required by the auditor in two key respects – **nature** and **pervasiveness** (ISA 705: paras. 2 and A1):

Nature of matter giving rise to the modification	Auditor's judgement about the pervasiveness of the effects or possible effects on the financial statements	
	Material but not pervasive	Material and pervasive
Financial statements are materially misstated (disagreement)	**Qualified opinion** ('except for...')	**Adverse opinion** ('the financial statements do not give a true and fair view...')
Inability to obtain sufficient appropriate audit evidence (limitation in scope)	**Qualified opinion** ('except for...')	**Disclaimer of opinion** ('we do not express an opinion...')

We learned earlier that the term **'material and pervasive'** has the following **definitions** and here they are in the context of selecting the most appropriate opinion, depending on its significance:

- Are **not confined** to **specific elements**, accounts or items of the financial statements

- If so confined, represent or could represent a **substantial proportion** of the financial statements

- In relation to disclosures, are **fundamental** to users' understanding of the financial statements.

  (ISA 705: para. 5(a))

Material misstatements (disagreements)

The circumstances leading to a modification due to material misstatement use the assessments of **materiality** already prepared during the audit and could include:

- The **appropriateness** of selected **accounting policies** (either inconsistent with the applicable financial reporting framework or those that do not lead to fair presentation)

- The **application** of selected accounting policies (either through inconsistency or error)

- The appropriateness or adequacy of **disclosures** in the financial statements.

  (ISA 705: para. 6)

Unable to obtain sufficient appropriate audit evidence (scope limitations)

The circumstances leading to a modification due to being unable to obtain sufficient appropriate audit evidence, are as follows:

- Circumstances **beyond the entity's control** (such as the loss of records in a fire)

- Circumstances relating to the **nature** or **timing of the auditor's work** (eg the auditor being appointed after the date of the inventory count)

- Limitations on the scope of the audit **imposed by management** (such as management denying access to third parties for external confirmations).

  (ISA 705: para. 6)

Activity 6: Audit opinions

You are the auditor for the external audit of Greenfingers Ltd for the year ended of 31 December 20X2.

On the evening of the year end inventory count at Greenfingers Ltd, the head gardener left a door to the store room open overnight, which meant that the heat regulation system failed and a large number of plants subsequently included in the inventory figure died.

These plants have been included in inventory at full value of £67,495 which is material to the financial statements. The finance director does not wish to amend the financial statements as he insists that the plants existed at the year end and therefore, it is fair to present that situation and recognise the loss in the next financial year.

Required

Assuming that the finance director does not amend the financial statements, select the most appropriate course of action for the auditor from the options below.

Take no action	Use an emphasis of matter paragraph	Issue a qualified opinion on the basis of insufficient appropriate evidence	Issue a qualified opinion on the basis of material misstatement

- Auditors can evaluate the progress they have made in completing the audit by reviewing audit documentation (or working papers) which are produced for a variety of purposes:
  - Demonstrating the findings from audit procedures
  - Demonstrating regulatory, ethical, legal and other compliance
  - Demonstrating best practice as a professional
  - Demonstrating the reasons for their judgement and conclusions

- Auditors then need to be able to deal with any matters arising from the audit appropriately – this includes understanding what to do in certain situations:
  - Evaluating misstatements identified during the course of the audit (using ISA 450)
  - Communicating audit findings with those charged with governance (TCWG) of an audited entity (using ISA 260)
  - Communicating deficiencies in internal control to those charged with governance and management (using ISA 265)

- Formal communication to those stakeholders who use the financial statements is undertaken by issuing the auditor's report, which has a specific format and layout under ISA 700:
  - Title and addressee
  - An opinion and the basis for that opinion
  - Disclosures relating to material uncertainty relating to going concern, key audit matters and other information
  - Responsibilities of both auditors and management
  - Regulatory issues
  - Date and signature of the auditor

- In some situations, the auditor's report may require some form of modification:
  - If a significant uncertainty exists, there may be a need for an additional form of communication within the auditor's report – this is called an emphasis of matter paragraph (ISA 706).
  - If the auditor cannot say that the financial statements give a true and fair view (or present fairly in all material respects) for some reason, both the reason and the extent need to be communicated via a modification to the auditor's opinion (qualified, adverse or disclaimer, as explained in ISA 705).

Keywords

- **Adverse opinion:** where the misstatement is both material and pervasive, leading the auditor to conclude that the financial statements "do not show a true and fair view"

- **Deficiency in internal control:** when a control is designed, implemented or operated in such a way that it is unable to prevent, or detect and correct, misstatements in the financial statements on a timely basis, or a necessary control is missing

- **Disclaimer of opinion:** where the shortage of evidence is both material and pervasive, leading the auditor to not give an opinion

- **Emphasis of matter:** paragraph draws users' attention to issues within the financial statements that they need to see in order to understand them properly

- **Qualified opinion:** where a matter that is material but not pervasive is identified by the auditor ("except for")

- **Significant:** in the auditor's opinion, those matters that warrant the attention of those charged with governance

- **Those charged with governance:** the directors of a company who are responsible for managing the company

- **Working papers:** the material prepared by and for, or obtained and retained by, the auditor in connection with the performance of the audit

1   State FOUR reasons why auditors need to prepare audit working papers.

2   Here is a completed internal control questionnaire about controls in the wages system at MEM.

Internal control questionnaire: MEM wages system		
Question	Y/N	Comment
Are personnel records kept for each member of staff containing details of wage rates?	Yes	Kept in wages office
Does a senior member of staff authorise new employees and changes in rates of pay?	Yes	Authorised by Richard Bishop or Mark Bishop
Are any changes in pay rates recorded in the personnel records?	Yes	By personnel director, Cathy
Are hours worked recorded on timesheets/ clocked?	Yes	Clock system in use
Is overtime approved by a senior member of staff?	Yes	Department heads review clock reports weekly
Are hours worked reviewed?	Yes	As above
Are wages reviewed against budget?	No	
Is a payroll prepared and approved before payment?	Yes	Prepared by Cathy, approved by Richard
Are total pay and deductions reconciled month on month?	Yes	
Where wages are paid in cash, is the wage cheque authorised?	N/A	
Is cash for wages payment kept securely?	N/A	
Is the identity of staff verified before cash payments are made?	N/A	
Are distributions of cash wages recorded?	N/A	
Are unclaimed wages kept securely?	N/A	
Where wages are paid by bank transfer, are transfer lists prepared and authorised?	Yes	Computer produces from payroll, Richard authorises
Are transfer lists compared to the payroll?	Yes	As above
Are details of deductions kept on employees' individual files?	Yes	

Internal control questionnaire: MEM wages system		
Question	**Y/N**	**Comment**
Are total pay and deductions reconciled month on month?	Yes	Computer highlights any discrepancies
Are costs of pay compared to budgets?	No	
Are gross pay and tax deducted per the payroll reconciled to returns made to the tax authorities?	Yes	Returns to tax office drafted from payroll by Cathy

Identify any deficiencies of the wages system at MEM and draft appropriate paragraphs to appear in a report to management concerning those control deficiencies, their consequences and suitable recommendations.

3   An audit client is in the middle of legal action with a former employee for sexual discrimination. If the employee wins the action, the company could have to pay compensation that would have a material impact on the financial statements.

Set out the implications of this legal action for the auditors.

4   For each of the following situations which have arisen in two unrelated audit clients, select whether or not the audit opinion on the financial statements would be modified.

The auditors have discovered aggregate misstatements of £25,000 on the audit of Spring Cleaners Ltd. Materiality has been set at £100,000. The directors refuse to amend the financial statements.	▼
March Hare Ltd's largest customer has gone into liquidation. The directors do not want to write off the debt owed by the customer which amounts to £25,000, which is material.	▼

Picklist:

Modified
Not modified

5   For each of the following situations which have arisen in two unrelated audit clients, select whether or not the auditor's opinion on the financial statements would be modified.

Gamma Ltd has included a warranty provision in the financial statements this year, having introduced a warranty to be offered to customers. The auditors have reviewed the warranty terms offered and believe the assumptions the provision is based on are, fundamentally, materially wrong.	▼
There is a significant uncertainty about Delta Ltd's ability to continue as a going concern. As the directors do not wish to make the situation any worse, they have not made any reference to going concern in the notes to the financial statements.	▼

Picklist:

Modified
Not modified

Activity answers

CHAPTER 1   Principles of auditing and professional ethics

Activity 1: Companies Act

Accounting records for transactions:	Income statement/Statement of profit or loss/Statement of profit or loss and other comprehensive income/Statement of cash flows
Accounting records for financial position:	Balance sheet/Statement of financial position
Matters in respect of which the receipt and expenditure takes place:	Revenue (including invoicing details of customers) Purchases (as above, with invoices for suppliers) Payroll (including employee records) Stock (inventory) Investment
Assets and liabilities:	Property, plant and equipment Vehicles Trading licences Cash Stock Provisions Loans Overdrafts
Statements of stock held by the company:	Results from stock count at warehouse, factory, third parties etc (raw materials, work in progress (WIP), finished goods etc)

Activity 2: Company concerns

Concerns about the directors of your company could be many and varied (such as 'Will they do a good job?', 'Could we have appointed someone better?' and 'Is our money safe?') but in broad terms, the concerns you have could be summed up by two phrases:

(1)   **Visibility** – as owners of the company, we employ directors for their entrepreneurial skills and their ability to make money, which is better than our own; hence their appointment. However, in order to allow them to concentrate on this, we must leave them alone to run and manage our company as they see fit. Decisions are taken and events occur without us being involved, meaning that we cannot always see how directors behave. This leads to the second concern:

(2) **Trust** – without any visibility of directors' actions and decisions, until the resultant outcomes become apparent, we must simply trust them to be doing the right thing.

These issues of trust and visibility are known as the **agency problem** – where agents (directors) are employed by principals (shareholders), there is always a risk that each party's interests might not be properly aligned and the company does not behave in the way intended by shareholders.

Activity 3: Assurance engagements

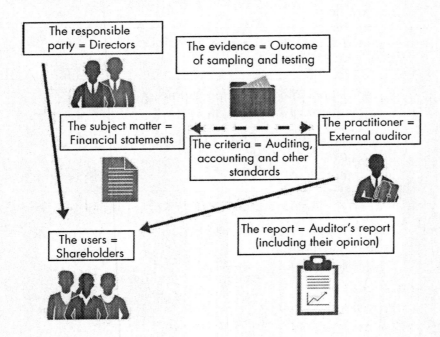

Activity 4: Duty of care

Company	Automatic
Bank	Must be proved
Individual shareholder	Must be proved
Creditor	Must be proved

The auditors do owe a duty of care to the client; that is, the shareholders as a body (the company) automatically under UK law. It is always possible that they may also owe a duty of care to other parties, such as the bank, individual shareholders and creditors, if those parties have established a special relationship with the auditors.

Activity 5: Types and levels of assurance

'In our opinion, the financial statements present fairly, in all material respects...'	Positive expression of assurance
This is provided as part of the auditor's opinion and is classed as high, but not absolute.	Reasonable assurance
This is not provided for an audit as it is only moderate and is insufficient for an audit.	Limited assurance
'Based on our review, nothing has come to our attention that causes us to believe that the financial statements are presented unfairly, in all material respects...'	Negative expression of assurance

The amount of work undertaken by auditors allows them to deliver reasonable assurance, expressed in a positive manner ('In our opinion...').

Other engagements (such as reviews) do not collect the same amount and quality of evidence as audits, so can only deliver limited assurance, which is a lower level of assurance than reasonable assurance. Consequently, these are expressed in a negative manner ('Based on our review, nothing has come to our attention...').

Activity 6: Fraud and error

The basic content of this answer comes directly from ISA 240 *The Auditor's Responsibilities Relating to Fraud in an Audit of Financial Statements*.

One **inherent limitation** of an audit is that some material misstatements might not be detected, even though the audit is properly planned and performed in line with ISAs – this is due to the **nature of fraud**, which differs from error due to **intent**.

Three conditions are usually necessary for fraud to exist: an ability to rationalise the fraudulent action (**dishonesty**); a perceived **opportunity** to commit fraud; and an incentive to commit fraud (**motive**).

Misstatement issues are more significant with fraud than error, due to the methods of **concealment** used by perpetrators (such as **forgery** and **deliberate failure to record transactions**). This can be exacerbated by **collusion** between parties who work to perpetuate a fraud by making evidence seem persuasive when, in fact, it is false.

Fraud is even more of an issue for auditors when **management** of an entity is involved, due to their ability to **manipulate** key accounting records. To counter such fraud, the auditor needs to maintain a sense of professional scepticism and remain alert to the threat of such management override of controls.

Activity 7: Fraud risk and professional scepticism

	Greater professional scepticism?	Lesser professional scepticism?
The finance director has requested that you complete the audit on time in order to meet head office reporting deadlines. The finance director has a profit-related bonus but has always accepted adjustments that you asked for on previous audits.		There is always a risk of managers trying to influence profit figures to increase their bonus, but this seems to be reasonable and does not add to your sense of scepticism.
The payroll officer has asked that you do not perform any testing of the payroll until she returns from her holiday. There are no other members of staff who can assist you with the payroll audit.	Such a case is classic fraud-masking behaviour. The fraud can be perpetrated and kept secret by one member of staff while they are present and kept secret while they are away, as no one will be looking at their work. This is evidence of a poor control environment as well, so casts some doubt on the integrity (or at least competence) of management.	
When reviewing the board minutes, you read that the company has applied for significant funding to support the currently poor cash flow. From recent conversations with the chief accountant, however, you were under the impression that revenue and cash flow were both healthy and that the company was performing well.	Such an oversight is not likely to be a simple accident, more likely an attempt to mislead the auditor – again, this is a symptom of a poor control environment and shows the integrity of management in a poor light.	

Activity 8: Fundamental ethical principles

Being dishonest about a business relationship with a client	Integrity
Accepting an engagement when not trained to complete it	Professional competence and due care
Insider trading by deciding to purchase a client's shares	Confidentiality

Activity 9: Ethical threats

	Tick
One client represents 25% of the audit firm's total fees for the year	✓
Representing an audit client in a tax investigation **Tutor note.** This is an example of an **advocacy** threat.	✗
Receiving free VIP tickets to the World Cup Final from a client. **Tutor note.** While this may appear to unduly influence the auditor, it does not represent an interest held, such as an investment of some sort. Due to this probably being a gift or some form of hospitality (maybe even a bribe?), it is an example of a **familiarity** threat.	✗

Activity 10: Ethical safeguards

Providing a valuation service to an audit client for assets held by a subsidiary of that client.	Use of different personnel with different reporting lines
Seven members of the audit firm own shares in the firm's audit clients. **Tutor note.** This is an example of a **firm-wide** safeguard as it does not relate to a specific engagement.	A register of interests and relationships between audit team members and clients
The audit manager's brother is promoted to become finance director of that client. **Tutor note.** Independent review of working papers would not be sufficient to address the familiarity risk so rotation is more appropriate here.	Rotation of senior personnel

BPP
LEARNING MEDIA

Activity 11: Confidentiality

	Tick
A request for information as part of a tax investigation	✓
A request for working papers from the incoming auditor during a competitive tender without receiving client approval **Tutor note.** Had the auditor received client approval, this would have been allowed.	✗
An external quality control review carried out by the FRC	✓

CHAPTER 2 Systems of internal control

Activity 1: Computer controls

- Passwords
- User names
- Usage log
- Firewalls
- Anti-virus software
- Authorisation codes
- Physical security
- Back-ups

Activity 2: Control activities

Performance reviews	Budgetary control meetings
Information processing	Agreeing the sales ledger total to a batch of authorised invoices
Physical controls	Security staff at a warehouse
Segregation of duties	Separate staff for counting, banking and recording cash

Activity 3: Internal control inherent limitations

Limitations of internal controls could occur in the following areas:

- Human error – human judgement can sometimes be faulty due to overconfidence, fatigue, stress etc. Such error can be traced back to either the design or implementation of a particular internal control.

- Human error might be experienced in the interpretation of results from reports produced by the internal control system (eg misinterpreting the results of an exception report).

- An entity may make a judgement on the amount of money that a control is designed to save, compared with the amount that such a control costs to implement (the so-called 'cost-benefit' argument). For this reason, many entities do not arrange insurance cover for all their assets, as the cost of such premiums would be prohibitive – instead, a fund is set up to cover potential losses.

- Fraud is one area already discussed where the limitations of internal control are very much exposed – collusion between two parties can circumvent segregation of duties controls, while management can choose to ignore the controls in place due to the authority they hold over their employees.

- Finally, due to the freak nature of some transactions, circumstances or events mean that no matter how well designed or implemented an internal control is, there is a risk of the control not being able to cope with such a random item. This can result in some form of loss for the entity, and may also highlight where an internal control can be improved.

Activity 4: Control objectives, risks and procedures – introduction

Observe post opening	Test of control
Safeguard blank purchase order forms	Control activity
Review numerical sequence of goods received notes	Test of control

Activity 5: Control objectives, risks and procedures for systems

Systems such as these are often very complex and there is never one perfect answer- please refer to the Appendix found at the end of Chapter 2 and compare what you have written with the examples provided.

Activity 6: Ascertaining the accounting system

Review of last year's working papers
Enquiries of client's staff
Review of policies and procedural manuals

Activity 7: Internal control questionnaire

Question	Yes/No	Comment
Are orders only accepted from low credit risks?	Yes	Sales staff ensure that customers have not exceeded their limits
Are despatches checked by appropriate personnel?	Yes	Ian Jones checks the order prior to despatch
Are goods sent out recorded?	Yes	Ian Jones raises a goods despatch note (GDN)
Are customers required to give evidence of receipt of goods?	Yes	They are required to sign and return a copy of the GDN
Are invoices checked to despatch notes and orders?	Yes	Agreed by Jane Hill
Are invoices prepared using authorised prices?	Yes	Sales department check to current price list
Are invoices checked to ensure they add up correctly?	No	Jane does not appear to complete additional work on invoices
Are sales receipts matched with invoices?	No	No mention of this check being carried out
Are statements sent out regularly?	Yes	Monthly
Are overdue accounts reviewed regularly?	No	Irrecoverable debts are rare so this check is not completed
Are there safeguards over post received to ensure that cheques are not intercepted?	No	No mention of what happens to them before they get to Beth Simpkins
Are bankings made daily?	No	Cheques are kept in the safe but banking is not regular
Would it be appropriate to perform tests of control here?	Yes	In general, the system of controls is sound, meaning that the auditor would test them to provide reliance on their sound operation. As a result of this there would be reduced amounts of substantive testing of revenue balances

Activity 8: Documenting systems

	Advantages	Disadvantages
Narrative notes	Quick to prepare	Confusing if system is complex
Flowcharts	Easier to interpret for larger, more complex systems	Need experience to prepare
Questionnaires	Easy to delegate to junior staff	Client may overstate controls

Activity 9: Evaluating systems

Task 1

Any five from the following:

- Sales staff check that outstanding orders are not in excess of the credit amount before taking orders

- Orders are recorded on pre-numbered sales orders

- Only Ted is allowed to authorise sales orders over £20,000

- Only Ted is allowed to authorise new customers after a credit check has been carried out

- Ian Mellor checks goods to be despatched for quantity and quality

- Invoices created from goods despatch notes and matching sales order

- Prices are automatically inserted on the invoice

- The production of invoices automatically triggers updating of the sales day book and ledger

- Post is opened by two people

- Processing the cash book automatically updates the sales ledger for receipts

- Marie Edgehill reconciles sales ledger control account on monthly basis

- Tessa Goodyear reviews an aged receivables report for potentially irrecoverable receivables weekly

Task 2

Only Ted Bishop is allowed to authorise new customers and orders over £20,000. ⬚ Potentially both ⬚

It is good that there is a control over larger purchases, but the fact that it is restricted to one person means that if Ted Bishop is ill or on holiday, customers may be kept waiting and ultimately lost, which is a weakness in the system.

Orders are recorded on pre-numbered sales orders. ⬚ Strength ⬚

Orders should not get lost and therefore be unfulfilled.

Goods are sometimes ready for despatch early. | Deficiency |

This suggests weaknesses in the system to determine when goods can be produced by and may mean that goods have to be stored on MEM's premises at MEM's risk until they can be despatched to the customer. It also adds to the delay between MEM spending money on raw materials and recouping money on sales. The initial prediction of production time should be more accurate.

It is necessary for Tessa to manually override the price system on the computer if a special price has been negotiated. | Deficiency |

This is a weakness as it means that the good controls over price input can be overridden for other reasons too. It might be better if the sales department set up any special prices agreed within the system and gave notice to Tessa of the appropriate code. However, controls would need to be exercised over this addition to standing data on the computer.

CHAPTER 3   Obtaining audit evidence

Activity 1: Controls and tests – purchases

Any five from the following:

Controls	Tests of control
Necessity for orders is evidenced prior to ordering and a requisition is raised.	Reviewed a sample of requisitions. Enquire about reorder levels with stores manager.
The company has a policy for choosing suppliers.	Review a sample of orders to ensure that the suppliers appear on the approved list.
Goods received are examined for quantity and quality.	Observe the stores' manager receiving some goods.
Goods received are checked against the order.	Observe the stores' manager receiving some goods. For those goods, scrutinise a sample of orders for evidence of the check.
Supplier invoices are checked to the order.	Observe the accounts assistant checking supplier invoices to the relevant order.
Supplier invoices are checked for prices; quantities and calculations are given a reference number.	Scrutinise a sample of supplier invoices for evidence of these checks.
Purchases are entered on the purchase ledger promptly.	Observe the accounts assistant posting the purchases invoices. Note the length of time between receiving and posting invoices.

Controls	Tests of control
Cheque requests are presented for approval with supporting documentation.	Scrutinise paid invoices for any evidence of approval. Observe the cheque payments routine.
Supplier statements are reconciled to the purchase ledger.	Scrutinise a sample of reconciliations. How are differences dealt with?
The purchase ledger control account is regularly reconciled with the purchase ledger list of balances.	Scrutinise a sample of reconciliations. Establish how differences are dealt with.

Activity 2: Controls and tests – payroll

Any four of the following:

Controls	Tests of control
Pieces worked are recorded.	Review records of pieces worked and test for accuracy.
Pieces worked are reviewed.	Scrutinise the exception report and look for evidence of authorisation.
Payroll is prepared by director.	Review payroll and check that it is indeed prepared by the director.
Identity of staff is verified prior to cash payments being made.	Attend a wages payout and observe the controls in operation.
The payroll master file (with details of office and administrative staff salaries) can only be accessed and amended by authorised individuals.	Interrogate the payroll master file to establish whether unauthorised staff can easily access or amend details.
Bank transfers, in respect of payroll, are made to the correct employee.	Compare a sample of automatic bank transfers made with bank account details provided by employees.

Activity 3: Controls or substantive?

Selection of ten invoices to test for correct authorisation in line with official signatory list	Test of control Substantive test
Tracing ten non-current assets back to initial purchases invoices to verify their value	Test of control Substantive test
Tracing ten non-current assets back to initial purchases invoices to verify they were allocated to the correct cost centre	Test of control Substantive test

As you can see from the last two examples, the same audit test can have both controls and substantive purposes behind them – this comes out of effective and efficient audit planning.

Activity 4: Ginger Ltd (1)

The correct answer is the **number of nights the hotel is open during the year**.

Workings

Substantive analytical procedures are used to verify an amount in total, so for Ginger $10 \times 55\% \times £75 \times 100 \times 365$ nights = £15,056,250 which proves the £15m revenue figure reported is materially correct.

The other pieces of information may be useful but will not help (we are told that £75 includes all charges, so bar and restaurant spend are not required). **Plus**, you cannot just assume 365 nights a year as there may have been closures in some of them during the year (hence, the 'no further information required' option is inappropriate).

Activity 5: Ginger Ltd (2)

Findings	Implications
The room rate of £50 now means that the revenue for Ginger should only be around £10 million – the financial statements are still recording £15 million.	The reported amount for revenue may be misstated. There may be elements of revenue that we are unaware of – we will need to perform further testing on revenue to ensure there are no flaws in any other assumptions (eg occupancy rate). We may have to consider the danger that management are attempting to manipulate the financial statements and should consider their integrity. We should inspect management accounts to verify the amounts recorded for revenue on a monthly basis. We may need to enquire whether there are any hotel premises or income streams that we were unaware of and establish if this changes any of our risk assessments or materiality calculations.

Activity 6: Mixed audit approach or substantive procedures only?

Scoot Ltd is a new company that has not been audited before and is dominated by its managing director and his informal operating style. Sales are of greatest importance to him as the company attempts to break into a competitive retail sector.	Substantive procedures only, with no tests of control
Whitney plc is an established listed company that operates in a stable market with strong governance procedures, including an audit committee.	Tests of control and substantive procedures
The board of Marine Ltd has just informed its external auditor that it wishes to replace its ledger systems due to a number of errors identified in its management accounts. **Tutor note.** This is not straightforward, but if the client is going to replace their systems, it is likely that they cannot currently be relied upon and therefore a purely substantive approach would be appropriate.	Substantive procedures only, with no tests of control

Activity 7: Assertions (1)

Select a sample of vehicles from the list of non-current assets and obtain their certificates of ownership. Seeking evidence of ownership proves that the entity has the **right** to include such assets within the financial statements (as well as any **obligations** that ownership would impose, such as maintenance).	Rights and obligations
Select a sample of receivables from the statement of financial position and agree to original invoices. The direction of testing is important here – you are testing from the statements to their source, which is a test that the figures **exists** (hence, testing for any **overstatement** of assets).	Existence
Select a sample of receivables from the sales ledger and agree to the final amount on the statement of financial position. The direction of testing is important again here – you are now testing from the source to the end statements, which is a test that all sales have been included and are **complete** (hence testing for any **understatement** of assets).	Completeness

Trace a selection of payments included in cost of sales to original invoices.	Occurrence
This is again a test of **overstatement** but this time it is for a **transaction**, so it is worth remembering that statement of profit or loss items are tested for **occurrence** while assets and liabilities are tested for **existence** (both can be reviewed for **completeness** when testing understatement).	

Activity 8: Assertions (2)

Testing cut-off for staff bonuses paid at the end of the financial year	Verifying bonus payments to payroll records to determine their timing
Confirming the accuracy of staff bonuses paid at the end of the financial year	Reconciling payroll records to a schedule of staff bonus payments authorised by the finance director
Confirming the value of cash investments held in a savings account by a client	Obtaining a letter from the bank stating the amount of savings held by the client

Activity 9: CAATs

Extraction of all receivables balances older than 120 days to perform irrecoverable receivable work	Audit software
Input of purchases invoices with false customer numbers to ensure that the system rejects the invoices	Test data
Comparison of suppliers on ledger with previous years to discover any new or missing suppliers	Audit software

Activity 10: Sampling (1)

Obtain evidence that sales have not been understated	Sales order
Obtain evidence that sales have not been overstated	Sales ledger

Activity 11: Sampling (2)

Auditors intend to increase reliance on the company's system of internal control for the purposes of the audit.	Increase
Auditors believe that there is likely to be a higher deviation rate in controls due to a new member of staff.	Increase
Increased activity in the factory and new customers, resulting in 25% more sales invoices being issued during the year.	No effect

CHAPTER 4   Planning: audit risk

Activity 1: Detection risk

(i)   5% = 50% × 20% × 50%

(ii)   5% = 50% × 40% × 25%

Detection risk is the risk that audit procedures do not detect a misstatement – it is logical that, in order to reduce this risk to a figure as close to zero as possible, the auditor must perform relatively more work; hence, reducing the risks of not detecting a misstatement, whether caused by fraud or error.

In the examples above, the second scenario shows a company where controls are half as good (or twice as risky) and, as such, we cannot rely on J Club's controls as much we did in scenario (i). In order to keep the risk of our firm giving an incorrect opinion to 5% with fewer controls to rely on, we therefore have to screen more transactions ourselves in the absence of J Club's own controls.

Had J Club's inherent risks changed, this would have affected our detection risk as well, in line with the equation, and potentially given us a different balancing figure.

Activity 2: Audit risk

If inherent and control risk have been determined to be high, auditors will have to carry out a high level of detailed testing to render overall audit risk acceptable.	True – as detection risk will need to be low, which means a high level of testing must be carried out.
The head of internal audit has just been suspended from one of your clients on suspicion of fraud. As a result, you assess that control risk has fallen.	False – being unable to trust the work of the internal auditor means that controls are less likely to be relied upon and as such control risk rises.

One of your largest retail clients has decided to cease taking cash at all its stores. You assess that inherent risk will fall for that client.	True – cash is an inherently risky item due to its portability and anonymity, so reducing the reliance on this as part of the client's business will mean the inherent risk of the audit falls.

Activity 3: IZK Ltd

IZK Ltd
Statement of financial position as at 30 September 20X6

	20X6 £	20X5 £
ASSETS		
Non-current assets		
Property, plant and equipment	46,595	41,675
Current assets		
Inventories	60,120	58,675
Trade and other receivables	140,674	124,968
Cash and cash equivalents	17,547	6,617
	218,341	190,260
Total assets	264,936	231,935
EQUITY AND LIABILITIES		
Equity		
Share capital	1,000	1,000
Retained earnings	184,187	142,039
	185,187	143,039
Non-current liabilities		
Bank loans	4,762	14,910
Current liabilities		
Trade and other payables	74,987	73,986
Total liabilities	79,749	88,896
Total equity and liabilities	264,936	231,935

The four balances most likely to need review from the statement of financial position would be property, plant and equipment, trade and other receivables, cash and cash equivalents and bank loans. Non-current assets are usually depreciated, so we would expect to see a fall in their value but in 20X6 they have increased – this is not unusual, but begs the question of how they could have increased when:

(a)   No revaluation reserve exists

(b)   No fresh share capital has been issued

(c)   Bank loans have fallen, suggesting that no new debt has been taken out (we may have seen a repayment of some debt, but see the next point)

(d)   Cash has risen, suggesting that cash balances were not used to redeem the bank loan. So how did the company afford new property, plant and equipment?

There are enough questions here to cause the auditor to be alerted to the risk of material misstatement in the statement of financial position – further audit procedures will then be prompted as a result of this basic analysis.

Activity 4: Bucket Ltd

Trade receivables has increased by 25% and revenue has increased by 7%	Overstated
Trade payables has decreased by 5% and purchases has increased by 4%	Understated

Activity 5: Material or not?

There is an error in receivables, value £7,500.	Material
A loan to a director has been disclosed in the financial statement at £2,000. Actually the correct sum is £2,010.	Material
The company is required to keep a current asset ratio of 2:1. An error of £100 has been found in receivables, which will cause the ratio to drop below this level.	Material

Activity 6: Materiality issues

Performance materiality should be set at less than materiality for the financial statements as a whole.	True
Materiality is a measure of the importance of items to a reader of financial statements.	True
Items may be material due to their size, nature or effect on the financial statements.	True
A building carried in the financial statements is judged to be 'material and pervasive' if it represents 70% of total assets and 150% of profit before tax and is subject to an impairment review due to extensive damage. It is the only premises of a trading company that cannot relocate due to commercial pressure. **Tutor note.** Determining whether something is 'material and pervasive' is usually going to require a degree of judgement by the auditor. However, in this case, it is probably more clear-cut as, although this relates to only one item, it represents a substantial proportion of the financial statements and the impairment is likely to substantially affect the future of the company.	True

CHAPTER 5   Planning: audit procedures

Activity 1: Risk of misstatement

The entity is to be sold and the purchase consideration will be determined as a multiple of reported profit.	Increase
The company has a history of being slow to follow new accounting standards and guidance.	Increase

Activity 2: Pebbles Ltd

Any four from:

- John White is considering selling his stake in the company. He therefore has an incentive to manipulate the figures in the accounts in order to achieve a better price for his shares.

- Sales are made on a cash basis. Cash held on the premises is susceptible to misappropriation and so may be difficult to substantiate in the financial statements.

- Inventory has a short shelf life. Any out of date inventory held at year end will need to be written off and may be overvalued in the financial statements.

- Casual staff may make errors when recording sales or misappropriate assets within the business, leading to errors within the financial statements.

- High staff turnover may result in misstatements in the payroll costs recorded in the financial statements.

- Leased premises may be accounted for incorrectly (for example, leased premises may not be treated in line with the most appropriate type of lease, leading to misstatements to both assets and liabilities).

Activity 3: JICS driving school

10 × Ford Fiestas
2 × PCs and monitors for the office
2 × desk telephones
10 × mobile telephones
Car insurance
Car servicing
Installation of dual controls in cars
Replacement tyre for car no. 6
Repairs to bumper of car no. 4
Office fixtures and fittings
'JICS' signs to go on top of cars

There is logic that certain expenditure is capitalised when servicing (literally) a non-current asset. However, **tyres** and **repairs** are generally regarded as fair wear and tear, so in practice they are referred to as revenue items.

Insurance and **servicing** are also classified as ongoing operating costs.

There may be a *de minimis* level for non-current assets to be created in order to keep such records manageable, so items like **desk telephones** may fall beneath this threshold and be lost within normal operating costs, but they are kept as non-current assets here for consistency.

Activity 4: Campey Ltd non-current assets

Completeness

(1) Compare non-current assets balance on general ledger with non-current asset register and reconcile any differences.

(2) Select a sample of non-current assets from knowledge of the business and trace them to the non-current asset register.

(3) Review any sensitive items within the statement of profit or loss, such as motoring expenses and building repairs, to ensure that items which should have been capitalised throughout the year have not been expensed instead.

Rights and obligations

(1) Review title deeds for land and buildings to confirm ownership.

(2) Review vehicle registration documents for a sample of company vehicles to confirm ownership.

(3) Review lease documentation to establish any finance lease obligations regarding non-current assets.

Existence

(1) Select a sample of assets from the non-current asset register and physically trace them to those assets.

(2) Inspect the assets to ensure that they exist, are in good order and are obviously being used by Campey Ltd.

Valuation

(1) As assets have not been revalued during the year, testing should start with additions. Confirm the amounts included at cost by reviewing the invoices for new vehicles and fittings.

(2) Recalculate the depreciation charge for a sample of assets.

(3) Review the bases for depreciation to ensure that 2% straight line for buildings, 25% diminishing balance for vehicles and 15% straight line for fittings are still reasonable.

(4) Use inspection evidence (from existence testing above) to confirm reasonableness of valuations for assets, especially impairments of land and buildings due to market conditions, dilapidation etc.

Activity 5: Paper Products Ltd

Before:

(i) Preparation

- Review working papers from the previous year
- Determine arrangements with management in advance
- Become familiar with nature of inventory
- Consider need for an expert
- Inventory held by/for third parties – review procedures to account for this
- Review client's count of physical inventory instructions. This should include the following:
  - In writing
  - Two independent counts
  - Systematic clearing of areas
  - Identification of obsolete damaged inventory
  - Supervision
  - Cut-off considered
  - Count sheets – pre-numbered, written in ink and controlled in distribution and collection
  - Investigation of differences – what happens if two counts disagree?

(ii)   Determine audit procedures required to cover a representative selection of inventory and inventory locations

(iii)   Identify potential problem/risk areas

During:

(i)   Review client staff – are they following the instructions?

(ii)   Test counts, from the physical inventory to the records and vice versa

(iii)   Note damaged, old and obsolete inventory for valuation purposes

(iv)   Review WIP for stage of completion

(v)   Inventory held by client for third parties must be excluded from count

(vi)   Take note of last goods received note (GRN) and goods despatch note (GDN)

(vii)   Form an overall impression of inventory levels/values

After:

(i)   Check sequence of inventory sheets

(ii)   Check client's computation of final inventory figure

(iii)   Trace own test count items through to inventory sheets

(iv)   Check replies from third parties

(v)   Inform management of general problems

(vi)   Follow up cut-off details

Activity 6: Inventory assertions

Test **Form an opinion of the condition of inventory and record any instances of damage or obsolescence.** **Result** There were 15 × 10m rolls of fabric stored near the roof of the warehouse where birds had nested, making the fabric unusable.	Valuation
Test **Trace 10 × 10m rolls of fabric from the inventory sheets to the relevant shelves of the warehouse.** **Result** All 10 rolls were found on the shelves in the locations specified by the main accounting system.	Existence

Test **Trace 10 x 10m rolls of fabric from the relevant shelves of the warehouse to the inventory sheets.** **Result** All 10 rolls were traced back to the list generated by the main accounting system.	Completeness
Test **Confirm that the fabric and garments held in the secure off-site storage facility are to be included in Glad Rags' inventory balance by verifying them to supporting documentation and invoices.** **Result** All rolls of fabric and garments were traced back to storage invoices and haulage records, confirming that they belong to Glad Rags.	Rights and obligations

Activity 7: Valuing inventory

General

Cast the inventory listing to establish that it is mathematically correct.

Confirm that an appropriate basis of valuation (first in first out) is being used, through a discussion with management.

Compare the gross profit percentage to the previous year or industry data.

Cost

For a sample of products, vouch the purchase prices to suppliers' invoices to ensure cost is correctly recorded on the inventory listing.

NRV

For a sample of inventory items held at the year end, obtain NRV by reviewing the post year end sales price.

Where NRV is lower than cost, ensure the items are written down to NRV.

Confirm that inventories are included at lower of cost and NRV in the financial statements.

Activity 8: Hodgson Ltd

(a) Record basis of valuation used in all three categories and ensure disclosure is accurate and inclusion in each category is appropriate.

(b) Test material costs (**all three categories**):

    (i) Trace back to individual invoices

    (ii) Ensure FIFO or appropriate bases being used

(iii) Review quantities used in WIP/finished goods

Test labour costs (**all three categories**):

(i) Trace calculations to supporting documentation (eg timesheets)

(ii) Review costing against actual labour and production statistics

Test application of overheads (**WIP** and **finished goods** only):

(i) Ensure only production overheads are included (and that standard costs are still appropriate)

(ii) Ensure based on normal activity levels

(c) Review stage of completion of **WIP**:

(i) Review for reasonableness of assumptions – consider physical inspection

(ii) Test calculations to ensure accurate

(d) Net realisable value of **finished goods**:

(i) Follow through items noted at inventory count

(ii) Review sales (volumes and prices) after year end

(iii) Review future orders to establish demand and likely sales prices

(iv) Consider any background knowledge obtained during the audit

(v) Establish extent of any write-downs from past year

(vi) Ensure any necessary adjustments to valuations have been made in light of this evidence (such as impairments to finished goods)

Activity 9: Cut-off testing

Revenues cut-off testing: **No further action/Refer to supervisor**

Purchases cut-off testing: **No further action/Refer to supervisor**

Regardless of whether the order from Terry's Threads was a regular order that came early or late, it has to be accounted for consistently and, as such, if it has been accounted for as inventory received before the year end, there must be a matching purchase cost and payable balance at the year end as well.

Activity 10: Circularisation

	Amount owed per sales ledger	Response from customer	Other information supplied by customer
British Clothes Stores plc	484,536	439,598	Cheque in post
IZK Ltd	74,973	74,973	n/a
Tisco Stores plc	78,805	71,663	Disputed invoice
J Club Ltd	323,024	323,024	n/a
Cavanaghs Ltd	14,388	nil	Goods not received yet
H and T Ltd	18,933	nil	Cheques in post
Nice Clothes Ltd	17,231	nil	Cheques in post
Ginger Ltd	22,315	22,315	n/a

Tisco is the only one where you cannot agree the balance yourself – those that agree (IZK, J Club and Ginger) need no further work, while British Clothes Stores, H and T and Nice Clothes have all paid their amounts owed and the only differences are due to timing (missing amounts have appeared in post year end cash receipts).

The warehouse records show that Cavanaghs' goods were despatched so they should be dealt with consistently, leaving the disputed invoice for Tisco. It is possible that their goods were not fully despatched or that some were damaged in transit – you need to perform more work on this before you can agree the balance as a valid trade receivable.

Activity 11: Pond Ltd

The following balances could be sampled:

Wed-Me Ltd	(8,429)
Astra Stones Ltd	Nil
Jewels 'r' Us Ltd	3,294
Magnifique Ltd	987

Other than size, you would test for collectability and any other risks – **Astra** having a nil balance might be correct, but you need to confirm this. Jewels 'r' Us and Magnifique are both overdue so should be investigated (and used to assess the company's allowance for doubtful debts) while any credit balance on the sales ledger should be investigated further.

Activity 12: Bank reconciliation

(a) Audit tests to be performed on the bank reconciliation:

Agree balance per cash book to cash book

Check arithmetic

Agree balance per bank statement on the reconciliation back to bank statement

Agree balance per bank statement back to bank letter

Vouch unpresented cheques and outstanding lodgements to after-date bank statements

Agree bank error to after-date statements and supporting documentation

Review bank letter for any undisclosed accounts

(b) Items to be referred to the audit supervisor:

Bank error

Items to be written off

Arithmetic

Disclosure items

Errors with source data

There are **two issues** that you may have spotted with this bank reconciliation – the **first** is that one of the outstanding cheques seems much older than the other two from their numbers, which might suggest a cheque that might never get presented and, as such, may require writing off the relevant accounts.

The **second** issue is that the bank reconciliation does not balance (£52,**296** vs £52,**926**). This could be due to a transposition error when producing the reconciliation or an error in the cash book or bank statement – both of which would need following up with the entity's staff.

Activity 13: HEC Ltd

The following work should be carried out on the loan:

*   Obtain a schedule showing what is due in more than one year and what is due in less than one year.

*   Test the calculations to ensure that this analysis is correct, that interest has been treated correctly and that the total balance payable agrees to the bank letter.

*   Ensure that appropriate disclosure has been made in the financial statements.

Activity 14: Gavilar Ltd

Objective	Suggested audit procedures
(a) Completeness	(i) Review trade payables using analytical procedures, comparing to previous year or budgets.
	(ii) Review goods received notes around the year end to ensure purchases have been correctly treated for cut-off purposes.
	(iii) Review unpaid invoice files for any liabilities not yet provided for.
	(iv) Review after-date payments for any liabilities not recorded.
	(v) Obtain a list of trade payables and reconcile to the financial statements.
(b) Rights and obligations	(i) Circularise trade payables (the procedure is similar to that used for trade receivables).
	(ii) Reconcile payables balances at the year end to a supplier's statement and follow up any discrepancies.
	Both these tests also provide evidence of completeness and valuation.
(c) Valuation	Ensure closing provisions/accruals are calculated in accordance with accounting policies and are consistent.
(d) Existence	(i) Circularise trade payable and/or reconcile using suppliers' statements.
	(ii) Perform cut-off tests on purchases and credit notes.
(e) Disclosure	Ensure trade payables have been properly analysed between those due in less than one year and those due in more than one year.

Other payables will include amounts due to be paid that do not form part of normal cost of sales (such as administration overheads, energy costs, rentals and insurance costs). In practice, they will not be treated any differently to trade payables but their patterns may be different, meaning that analytical procedures need to take this into account.

Activity 15: Adjustments

The auditor has found an invoice for office supplies ordered and delivered on the last day of the financial year. The invoice amount has not been included in the total for purchases in the statement of profit or loss. The amount for these supplies is material.	Requires to be adjusted
The auditor has completed analytical review of the cost of sales for a bakery. This analysis has indicated that ingredient costs per loaf have increased from 12.8 pence in the previous year to a figure closer to £3.56 per loaf. The non-financial information on the numbers of loaves has been corroborated during the audit.	Requires to be adjusted
The auditor has selected 20 payments from the purchase ledger total and has been tracing them back to invoices for evidence of both existence and valuation. Of these 20 payments, 19 have been traced successfully back for both assertions. The 20th item has no invoice and relates to health and safety assessments carried out at the entity's head office. A similar amount was included in last year's statement of profit or loss and this year's figure can be agreed back to a quotation that the chief accountant was sent by the contractor. The audit senior has recorded evidence of this assessment within the current file as part of the firm's wider audit testing.	Does not require to be adjusted

The third example is far from clear-cut without any materiality or risk assessments to refer to, but is an example of how the auditor looks for **corroborative evidence** that seems **plausible**. In this example, although we have no back-up for this payment, a matching quotation was issued and the amount is both ongoing and consistent with what the auditors understand of the entity; hence, both **valuation** and **existence** have some **persuasive evidence**, rather than being **conclusive**.

In such a case, it is probable that the weight of evidence is stacked in the entity's favour and the auditor's opinion (note – this is **not** a guarantee) is likely to be that the financial statements are free from material misstatement.

Activity 16: Miscellaneous procedures

Consider the effect of any price rises during the year.	Cash sales from a retail outlet
Review sales ledger for old receivables which are still unpaid.	An allowance for a doubtful debt
Verify amount outstanding by reference to subsequent payments.	An accrual for an unpaid electricity bill
Perform analytical procedures by comparing payments with previous years to see if they appear reasonable.	A prepaid insurance premium
Recalculate amounts due in relation to tax and national insurance payable by employees.	Deductions paid to HM Revenue & Customs (HMRC)

CHAPTER 6 Evaluation

Activity 1: Documentation

- Assisting the audit team to plan and perform the audit (by reference to the original planning documents produced when the audit was agreed with the client)

- Assisting with the review and supervision responsibilities carried out by members of the audit team to ensure quality control

- Ensuring that the audit team is accountable for its work and that anyone not working on the audit team can understand what occurred during the audit

- Retaining a record of matters of continuing significance to future audits, including discussions with client management and those charged with governance, as well as any inconsistencies discovered during the audit

- Allowing internal inspection through systems of quality control review

- Allowing external inspections in accordance with legal, regulatory and other requirements

230

Activity 2: Working papers

Working paper	Reason for preparation
A register of shares in audit client companies owned by staff members	Demonstrating legal, regulatory and ethical compliance by the auditor
A copy of an email sent by the finance director of Curtis Ltd explaining a bid that has been made to acquire the company	Recording matters from an audit that are either unusual or significant
Briefing notes for the audit team before the start of the audit of Gordon Ltd	Planning, directing, supervision and review of the audit engagement
A reconciliation of circularised responses to a list of receivables for an audit client	Supporting audit evidence for the auditor's opinion

Tutor note. Although each option was used here, and each was only used once, you should be prepared for some answer options in your assessment to be used either more than once or not at all.

Activity 3: Glad Rags

When reviewing the bank statements, the chief accountant removed some of the pages relating to the period of time after the year end. This could be a sign that there are integrity issues with the chief accountant which the audit junior should pass on to the audit supervisor.	No further action Refer it to the supervisor
During his review of the payroll system, incorrect PAYE income tax rates were found to have been used. This was retrospectively corrected for the following month and all supporting transactions reviewed by the junior.	No further action Refer it to the supervisor

Activity 4: Reporting recommendations

Deficiency	**Deficiency**
When invoices are raised, they are not reviewed to ensure that additions are correct.	Post opening procedures appear unsupervised with no list of initial receipts – customer remittance information does not appear to be retained.
Consequence	**Consequence**
Invoices could be overstated (leading to loss of goodwill from customers) or understated (leading to a loss of funds for the company).	Receipts could be misappropriated or lost once at the company. Funds might not be effectively allocated against the correct customer, leading to incorrect records on outstanding amounts and irrecoverable debts.
Recommendation	**Recommendation**
Invoices should be checked for additions prior to being sent out to customers for correct additions and VAT. This should be done by someone other than Jane (eg Beth) to introduce a second pair of eyes.	A list of all receipts should be created on opening each item of post for completion purposes and all customer remittances retained and attached to cheques.

Activity 5: Emphasis of matter paragraphs

You are the auditor for a supermarket. A customer has eaten own-brand produce and suffered an allergic reaction to one of the ingredients. The customer is currently claiming punitive damages for insufficient information on the food label. If successful, the damages would represent a material amount to the company. The company was successfully sued for a similar event three years ago, so has created a provision for this and has disclosed the matter in full in its financial statements.	Unmodified opinion with emphasis of matter paragraph Unmodified opinion with no further modification to the audit report

The course of action suggested here seems reasonable as the client has done what seems prudent, given that it seems likely to be unsuccessful in this case.

Activity 6: Audit opinions

Take no action	Use an emphasis of matter paragraph	Issue a qualified opinion on the basis of insufficient appropriate evidence	Issue a qualified opinion on the basis of material misstatement

The finance director is incorrect as the inventory was impaired before the year end. This could be called into dispute if the inventory count occurred on the very last day of the reporting period and the plants died after midnight – we know from the activity that the year end of Greenfingers Ltd is 31 December, so the inventory count may not have been carried out on New Year's Eve! You can expect the real assessment to be more specific and not introduce too much conjecture.

Assuming that the inventory was impaired, and the finance director chooses not to amend the financial statements for this material amount, the statements are materially misstated and a qualified opinion is appropriate.

Test your learning: answers

CHAPTER 1 Principles of auditing and professional ethics

1 A **company** is an **entity** registered as such under the Companies Act 2006.

2 It must be managed by its owners. ☑

A company does not have to be managed by its owners. However, registering a company does mean that it is seen as a separate entity from its owners, and that it must satisfy certain requirements of the Companies Act, such as keeping accounting records and having its financial statements audited.

3

Companies must keep records that disclose with reasonable accuracy the company's position at any time.	True
All companies must keep records of inventory. Only those companies that deal in goods need to fulfil this requirement (other companies have no stock/inventory to record).	False

4 An **audit** is an exercise carried out by **auditors** to ascertain whether the **financial statements** prepared by the **directors** are (in the UK) in accordance with UK GAAP and the **Companies Act 2006** and give what is known as a **true and fair view** .

5

Auditors are required to report on the truth and fairness of financial statements.	True
Auditors have a right of access to a company's books and records at any time.	True
Auditors are entitled to obtain explanations from the officers of a company.	True

6 The client and any other parties with whom they have implied a special relationship ☑

7 A duty of care existed, it was breached, causing loss.

8 **Confidentiality** is the duty to keep **client** affairs **private** .

9   The auditors must keep their work secure, so that they can keep client affairs private.

10   The audit firm's money laundering reporting officer ✓

CHAPTER 2   Systems of internal control

1   Internal control is the process **designed**, implemented and **maintained** by **those charged with governance**, **management** and other personnel to provide **reasonable assurance** about the achievement of the entity's **objectives** with regard to the reliability of **financial reporting**, effectiveness and efficiency of **operations** and compliance with applicable laws and regulations.

2

A company should only pay for work done by employees.	Control objective
Company vehicles are used by employees for their own purposes.	Risk
Part C39t99, in regular use in the business, is reordered when inventory levels fall below 200.	Control procedure

3

The directors can ensure a good control environment by implementing controls themselves and never bypassing them.	True
The directors should not assign authority for control areas to members of staff.	False
A good control environment always leads to a good system of control overall.	False

A good control environment would usually suggest that the control system is strong, but this is not always the case. The directors or management who are charged with governance within the entity should maintain overall authority over the design and implementation of controls. This function should not be delegated to members of staff.

4   A large company is more likely to have a good control environment than a small company. ☑

Control environment depends on the attitudes, awareness and actions of directors. Although some small companies may have difficulties in activating controls such as segregation of duties due to staff restrictions, the attitudes of management will not necessarily be poorer just because the company is small.

In practice, control activities will be similar in all sizes of company over core activities, although all companies differ and have some varying objectives, so controls will alter from company to company to some extent. Large and small companies are likely to be different in terms of the formality of their control environment, or the formality and extent of their information systems.

5   Who monitors controls depends on the size of the company and its personnel: it may be an internal audit function, but it could also be the directors, or department heads. ☑

Who monitors controls will vary from company to company. Larger companies may have internal audit functions, one of whose key purposes will be to monitor controls. In small companies, control monitoring is less likely to be formal and is likely to be carried out by the staff in charge of each function or department.

6   Control objectives over wages:

(1)   Employees only paid for work done
(2)   Gross pay calculated correctly and authorised
(3)   Gross pay, net pay and deductions correctly recorded on payroll
(4)   Wages and salaries paid recorded properly in bank records
(5)   Wages and salaries recorded correctly in the general ledger
(6)   Deductions calculated correctly and authorised
(7)   The correct amounts paid to the taxation authorities

7

Internal control procedure	
The payroll should be reconciled to other records, such as the cash payment for net pay per the bank's records.	Gross pay, net pay and deductions should be correctly recorded on payroll.
The payroll should be authorised by someone other than the personnel director.	Gross pay should be calculated correctly and authorised.

8

Internal control procedure	
Non-current assets are inspected regularly.	Assets are not maintained properly for use in the business.
Capital expenditure is approved by the purchasing director on behalf of the board.	Assets are bought from inappropriate suppliers at inflated cost.

9

Internal control procedure	
Inventory store is kept locked.	Inventory is stolen.
Goods inwards are checked for quality.	Damaged inventory is valued in the financial statements.

10

A series of questions designed to identify controls in a system. A 'no' answer indicates a deficiency in controls	Internal Control Questionnaire
A graphic rendition of the system, using conventional symbols to represent controls and documents	Flowchart

CHAPTER 3 Obtaining audit evidence

1

Existence	Account balances
Accuracy, valuation and allocation	Account balances
Cut-off	Classes of transaction

2 All sampling units should have an equal chance of being selected for testing.
☑

The other statements are all untrue.

3

Simran has been asked to select a sample of 12 sales invoices to trace from sales order to general ledger. There are 16 folders of sales orders for the year, stored in the sales office.	Haphazard – where there is such a large population, Simran should select on a haphazard basis
Julie has been asked to select a sample of 5 purchase ledger accounts to carry out a supplier statement reconciliation. There are 16 purchase ledger accounts.	Systematic – where there is a small population, ordered in a way that does not bias the sample (for example, alphabetically), systematic selection is suitable
Ben is selecting a sample of inventory lines to perform a valuation test. The audit team have been instructed to use the computerised techniques available to them, one of which is a sample selection program.	Random – if a random numbers program is available, it could be used as a suitable method of selecting a non-biased sample

4

Increase in the auditor's assessment of the risk of material misstatement	Increase
Increase in tolerable misstatement	Decrease
Decision to stratify a large population	Decrease

5   Computer assisted audit techniques are methods of obtaining **evidence** by using **computers.**

Audit software is **software** that can check **data** on computer systems by **interrogating** or by comparing versions of **programs** .

Test data is a way of checking computer **programming** by inputting real or false information and observing how the program deals with it.

CHAPTER 4   Planning: audit risk

1   The auditors must gain an understanding of industry, regulatory and other external factors, nature of the entity (including selection of accounting policies), objectives and strategies and business risks, performance measurement, and the internal control system.

2   In order to be able to assess risks ✓

This will then direct auditors as to what to test and how.

3   **Audit** risk is the risk that the auditors give an **inappropriate** opinion on the financial statements.

Control risk is the risk that the entity's internal control system will not prevent or detect and correct errors.

Inherent risk is the risk that items will be misstated due to their **nature** or due to their **context** .

Detection risk is the risk that errors will exist in financial statements and the auditors will not discover them.

4

Auditors cannot affect inherent and control risk as inherent and control risks are the risks that errors will arise in the financial statements as a result of control problems or the nature of items in the financial statements of the entity. The auditors cannot control those factors.	True
If inherent and control risk are high, detection risk should be rendered low to come to an overall acceptable level of risk. In order for detection risk to be low, the auditors will have to carry out a low level of testing.	False – detection risk should be low, but to achieve that auditors should carry out a high level of testing

5

The control environment is weak and there is considerable pressure on management to improve results year on year.	Increase
Management has implemented improvements in controls as a result of weaknesses identified last year.	Reduce

6

Materiality is the concept of significance to users of the financial statements.	True
Performance materiality will usually be higher than materiality assessed for the financial statements as a whole.	False – it will be lower

7

The company has diversified its operations during the year.	Increase
The company has discontinued operations in its riskiest operating area during the year.	Increase – although it might seem as though this would reduce risk, in this year, the company will have to meet accounting requirements relating to the changes, which increases audit risk

CHAPTER 5   Planning: audit procedures

1

Inventory is difficult to audit because it often consists of a large number of low value items which are collectively material.	True
Key assertions to test in relation to inventory are existence, completeness and valuation.	True

2

It is important to record cut-off correctly so that assets are not double counted (receivables and inventory).	True
It is important to record cut-off correctly so that a liability is not omitted in respect of an asset (payables and inventory).	True
For the purposes of the financial statements, it does not matter if the company misstates cut-off between raw materials and work in progress.	False

3

Obtain evidence of the value of raw material	Purchase invoice
Obtain evidence of the value of finished goods	Both – finished goods will be tested for purchase price, cost of conversion, and also net realisable value (hence testing to after-date sales invoices)

4   Net realisable value is tested with reference to after the year end **sales**. The value of items of inventory is compared to post year end **sales**. This is to ensure that inventory value is equal to or **lower** than net realisable value of the inventory.

5

Attending an inventory count	Existence
Tracing counted items to final inventory sheets	Completeness
Reviewing after year end sales invoices	Valuation

6   Auditors are concerned with completeness, existence, rights and obligations and valuation. ☑

7

Receivables circularisation	Rights and obligations – customers might agree that a debt is owed, but be unable to pay it
Reviewing sales receipts after year end	Both – looking at receipts after-date confirms valuation and that the company was owed that debt in the first place

8   Auditors usually rely 100% on controls over revenue by carrying out only controls testing. ☑

This is incorrect as revenue is almost certainly a material balance, which must be subject to some detailed testing (which may be analytical procedures only or tests of detail or a combination). Auditors may choose not to test controls at all if they appear weak.

9

Bank letter requests are sent out by the auditor directly to the bank.	True – although the bank will only reply if the client has given them permission to
Bank letter requests should be made at the year end date.	False – requests should be made about a month in advance of the year end to allow the bank time to process it
Auditors will commonly test cash balances even if they are not material.	True – because cash is highly susceptible to fraud

10 Auditors are concerned with completeness, existence and obligations. ☑

11

They represent a better source of evidence than replies to a receivables circularisation as they are sent direct to the company.	False – this reduces their value as potentially they could be tampered with but they still represent a good source of third-party evidence
They are only used when the auditor is unable to do a payables circularisation.	False – an auditor would only carry out a payables circularisation in exceptional circumstances
Testing supplier statements provides evidence that trade payables have not been understated.	True

12 Auditors should consider that payables might be **understated** and therefore not simply select large balances to test (although they must select **material** items). **Nil** balances should also be incorporated into the test.

13 **Accruals** are liabilities other than **trade** that arise because the company has received a benefit it has not yet paid for.

Non-current liabilities are loans repayable at a date **more than** one year after the year end.

14 Auditors are concerned with occurrence, accuracy and completeness. ☑

15 Accruals at a manufacturer

A manufacturer is likely to have the following accruals:

Wages – if wages are paid in arrears	Should be a month's payroll, which can be agreed to the payroll.
PAYE	This should also agree to the payroll as it should be a month's deductions. It can also be verified to the after-date payment.
VAT – if the VAT returns are not coterminous with the year end	This should be verifiable to the next VAT return.
Utilities	The company is likely to have paid standing charges for items such as gas, electricity and water in advance. These can be verified to the relevant invoices.

CHAPTER 6 Evaluation

1   Choose any four of the following:

- A record of audit evidence collected
- Support for any decision made about the auditor's opinion
- Demonstration of best practice (legal, ethical, professional and regulatory)
- Protection for the firm in the case of litigation (such as negligence)
- Planning, direction, supervision and review of any audit engagement
- A record of any contentious or significant issues identified during the course of the audit

2   **Deficiency: Failure to compare actual payroll costs to budget**

No one compares the cost of the payroll (wages, salaries, costs of employers' NI, any company pension contributions) to the budgeted cost at the start of the year.

Consequence

Errors may arise in the payroll (which could be highlighted by such comparison) and not be corrected which might result in overpayment of wages or of tax.

Recommendation

The payroll costs should be compared to budget on a monthly basis and variances investigated. The review should probably be carried out by Richard Bishop when he approves the payroll, although variance investigation could be carried out by someone else. This person should be someone other than Cathy to restrict opportunity for payroll fraud.

3   The auditors need to consider the implications of the litigation on the financial statements on:

- Potential provision or disclosure required for the compensation

- Potential impact on going concern if the litigation gives ground for further claims

4

The auditors have discovered aggregate misstatements of £25,000 on the audit of Spring Cleaners Ltd. Materiality has been set at £100,000. The directors refuse to amend the financial statements.	Not modified
March Hare Ltd's largest customer has gone into liquidation. The directors do not want to write off the debt owed by the customer which amounts to £25,000, which is material.	Modified

5

Gamma Ltd has included a warranty provision in the financial statements this year, having introduced a warranty to be offered to customers. The auditors have reviewed the warranty terms offered and believe the assumptions the provision is based on are, fundamentally, materially wrong.	Modified – this is a material misstatement resulting from an accounting policy.
There is a significant uncertainty about Delta Ltd's ability to continue as a going concern. As the directors do not wish to make the situation any worse, they have not made any reference to going concern in the notes to the financial statements.	Modified – for non-disclosure of the significant uncertainty about going concern.

Glossary of terms

It is useful to be familiar with interchangeable terminology including IFRS and UK GAAP (generally accepted accounting principles).

Below is a short list of the most important terms you are likely to use or come across, together with their international and UK equivalents.

UK term	International term
Profit and loss account	**Statement of profit or loss (or statement of profit or loss and other comprehensive income)**
Turnover or Sales	Revenue or Sales revenue
Operating profit	Profit from operations
Reducing balance depreciation	Diminishing balance depreciation
Depreciation/depreciation expense(s)	Depreciation charge(s)
Balance sheet	**Statement of financial position**
Fixed assets	Non-current assets
Net book value	Carrying amount
Tangible assets	Property, plant and equipment
Stocks	Inventories
Trade debtors or Debtors	Trade receivables
Prepayments	Other receivables
Debtors and prepayments	Trade and other receivables
Cash at bank and in hand	Cash and cash equivalents
Long-term liabilities	Non-current liabilities
Trade creditors or creditors	Trade payables
Accruals	Other payables
Creditors and accruals	Trade and other payables
Capital and reserves	Equity (limited companies)
Profit and loss balance	Retained earnings
Cash flow statement	**Statement of cash flows**

Accountants often have a tendency to use several phrases to describe the same thing! Some of these are listed below:

Different terms for the same thing
Nominal ledger, main ledger or general ledger
Subsidiary ledgers, memorandum ledgers
Subsidiary (sales) ledger, sales ledger
Subsidiary (purchase) ledger, purchase ledger

Bibliography

Companies Act 2006. (2006) SI 2006/46. Available from: http://www.legislation.gov.uk/ukpga/2006/46/contents [Accessed June 2017].

Department for Business, Innovation and Skills. (2016) *Small Companies Audit Exemption Thresholds: Written statement - HCWS491.* Available from: http://www.parliament.uk/business/publications/written-questions-answers-statements/written-statement/Commons/2016-01-26/HCWS491/ [Accessed June 2017].

Financial Reporting Council. (2010) Practice Note 16 *Bank Reports for audit purposes in the United Kingdom* (2010). London, FRC.

International Accounting Standards Board. (2003) IAS 2 *Inventories.* In *International Financial Reporting Standards* (2014). Available from: http://eifrs.ifrs.org [Accessed June 2017].

International Accounting Standards Board. (2010) IAS 17 *Leases.* In *International Financial Reporting Standards* (2014). Available from: http://eifrs.ifrs.org [Accessed June 2017].

International Accounting Standards Board. (2005) IAS 37 *Provisions, Contingent Liabilities and Contingent Assets.* In *International Financial Reporting Standards* (2014). Available from: http://eifrs.ifrs.org [Accessed June 2017].

International Auditing and Assurance Standards Board (2015) ISA 200 *Overall Objectives of the Independent Auditor of an Audit in Accordance with International Standards on Auditing.* New York, IAASB. Available from: http://www.ifac.org/publications-resources/2015-handbook-international-quality-control-auditing-review-other-assurance [Accessed 6 June 2017].

International Auditing and Assurance Standards Board. (2015) ISA 230 (redrafted) *Audit Documentation.* New York, IAASB. Available from: http://www.ifac.org/publications-resources/2015-handbook-international-quality-control-auditing-review-other-assurance [Accessed 6 June 2017].

International Auditing and Assurance Standards Board. (2015) ISA 240 *The Auditor's Responsibilities Relating to Fraud in an Audit of Financial Statements.* New York, IAASB. Available from: http://www.ifac.org/publications-resources/2015-handbook-international-quality-control-auditing-review-other-assurance [Accessed 6 June 2017].

International Auditing and Assurance Standards Board. (2015) ISA 250 *Consideration of Laws and Regulations in an Audit of Financial Statements.* New York, IAASB. Available from: http://www.ifac.org/publications-resources/2015-handbook-international-quality-control-auditing-review-other-assurance [Accessed 6 June 2017].

International Auditing and Assurance Standards Board. (2015) ISA 260 *Communicating with those Charged with Governance.* New York, IAASB. Available from: http://www.ifac.org/publications-resources/2015-handbook-international-quality-control-auditing-review-other-assurance [Accessed 6 June 2017].

International Auditing and Assurance Standards Board. (2015) ISA 265 *Communicating Deficiencies in Internal Control to those Charged with Governance and Management.* New York, IAASB. Available from: http://www.ifac.org/publications-resources/2015-handbook-international-quality-control-auditing-review-other-assurance [Accessed 6 June 2017].

International Auditing and Assurance Standards Board. (2015) ISA 315 (Revised) *Identifying and Assessing the Risks of Material Misstatement through Understanding the Entity and its Environment.* New York, IAASB. Available from: http://www.ifac.org/publications-resources/2015-handbook-international-quality-control-auditing-review-other-assurance [Accessed 6 June 2017].

International Auditing and Assurance Standards Board. (2015) ISA 320 *Materiality in Planning and Performing an Audit.* New York, IAASB. Available from: http://www.ifac.org/publications-resources/2015-handbook-international-quality-control-auditing-review-other-assurance [Accessed 6 June 2017].

International Auditing and Assurance Standards Board. (2015) ISA 450 *Evaluation of Misstatements Identified During the Audit.* New York, IAASB. Available from: http://www.ifac.org/publications-resources/2015-handbook-international-quality-control-auditing-review-other-assurance [Accessed 6 June 2017].

International Auditing and Assurance Standards Board. (2015) ISA 500 *Audit Evidence.* New York, IAASB. Available from: http://www.ifac.org/publications-resources/2015-handbook-international-quality-control-auditing-review-other-assurance [Accessed 6 June 2017].

International Auditing and Assurance Standards Board. (2015) ISA 520 *Analytical Procedures.* New York, IAASB. Available from: http://www.ifac.org/publications-resources/2015-handbook-international-quality-control-auditing-review-other-assurance [Accessed 6 June 2017].

International Auditing and Assurance Standards Board. (2015) ISA 530 *Audit Sampling.* New York, IAASB. Available from: http://www.ifac.org/publications-resources/2015-handbook-international-quality-control-auditing-review-other-assurance [Accessed 6 June 2017].

International Auditing and Assurance Standards Board. (2015) ISA 540 *Auditing Accounting Estimates, Including Fair Value Accounting Estimates and Related Disclosures.* New York, IAASB. Available from: http://www.ifac.org/publications-resources/2015-handbook-international-quality-control-auditing-review-other-assurance [Accessed 6 June 2017].

International Auditing and Assurance Standards Board. (2015) ISA 580 *Written Representations.* New York, IAASB. Available from: http://www.ifac.org/publications-resources/2015-handbook-international-quality-control-auditing-review-other-assurance [Accessed 6 June 2017].

International Auditing and Assurance Standards Board. (2015) ISA 700 (Revised) *Forming an Opinion and Reporting on Financial Statements.* New York, IAASB. Available from: http://www.ifac.org/publications-resources/international-standard-auditing-isa-700-revised-forming-opinion-and-reporting [Accessed 6 June 2017].

International Auditing and Assurance Standards Board. (2015) ISA 701 *Communicating Key Audit Matters in the Independent Auditor's Report.* New York, IAASB. Available from: http://www.ifac.org/publications-resources/international-standard-auditing-isa-701-new-communicating-key-audit-matters-i [Accessed 6 June 2017].

International Auditing and Assurance Standards Board. (2015) ISA 705 (Revised) *Modifications to the Opinion in the Independent Auditor's Report.* New York, IAASB. Available from: http://www.ifac.org/publications-resources/international-standard-auditing-isa-705-revised-modifications-opinion-indepen [Accessed 6 June 2017].

International Auditing and Assurance Standards Board. (2015) ISA 706 (Revised) *Emphasis of Matter Paragraphs and Other Matter Paragraphs in the Independent Auditor's Report.* New York, IAASB. Available from: http://www.ifac.org/publications-resources/international-standard-auditing-isa-706-revised-emphasis-matter-paragraphs-an [Accessed 6 June 2017].

Proceeds of Crime Act. (2002) SI 2002/29.
Available from: http://www.legislation.gov.uk/ukpga/2002/29/contents [Accessed June 2017].

Index

W

CRAVEN COLLEGE

REVIEW FORM

How have you used this Course Book?
(Tick one box only)

☐ Self study

☐ On a course_____

☐ Other _____

Why did you decide to purchase this Course Book? *(Tick one box only)*

☐ Have used BPP materials in the past

☐ Recommendation by friend/colleague

☐ Recommendation by a college lecturer

☐ Saw advertising

☐ Other _____

During the past six months do you recall seeing/receiving either of the following?
(Tick as many boxes as are relevant)

☐ Our advertisement in Accounting Technician

☐ Our Publishing Catalogue

Which (if any) aspects of our advertising do you think are useful?
(Tick as many boxes as are relevant)

☐ Prices and publication dates of new editions

☐ Information on Course Book content

☐ Details of our free online offering

☐ None of the above

Your ratings, comments and suggestions would be appreciated on the following areas of this Course Book.

	Very useful	Useful	Not useful
Chapter overviews	☐	☐	☐
Introductory section	☐	☐	☐
Quality of explanations	☐	☐	☐
Illustrations	☐	☐	☐
Chapter activities	☐	☐	☐
Test your learning	☐	☐	☐
Keywords	☐	☐	☐

	Excellent	Good	Adequate	Poor
Overall opinion of this Course Book	☐	☐	☐	☐

Do you intend to continue using BPP Products?   ☐ Yes ☐ No

Please note any further comments and suggestions/errors on the reverse of this page. The BPP author of this edition can be emailed at: lmfeedback@bpp.com

Alternatively, the Head of Programme of this edition can be emailed at: nisarahmed@bpp.com

REVIEW FORM (continued)

TELL US WHAT YOU THINK

Please note any further comments and suggestions/errors below

PARK LEARNING CENTRE
The Park Cheltenham
Gloucestershire GL50 2RH
Telephone: 01242 714333

UNIVERSITY OF
GLOUCESTERSHIRE
at Cheltenham and Gloucester

NORMAL LOAN